John and Mary;
or, The Fugitive Slaves,
a Tale of South-Eastern Pennsylvania:

By

Ellwood Griest

JOHN AND MARY;

OR,

THE FUGITIVE SLAVES,

A Tale of

SOUTH-EASTERN PENNSYLVANIA.

By ELLWOOD GRIEST.

WRITTEN ORIGINALLY FOR THE LANCASTER INQUIRER.

LANCASTER, PA.:
INQUIRER PRINTING AND PUBLISHING COMPANY.
1873.

PREPARED FOR PUBLICATION
BY
HISTORIC PUBLISHING

JOHN AND MARY; OR, THE FUGITIVE SLAVES, A Tale of SOUTH-EASTERN PENNSYLVANIA.

By

ELLWOOD GRIEST.

WRITTEN ORIGINALLY FOR THE *LANCASTER INQUIRER*.

LANCASTER, PA.:
INQUIRER PRINTING AND PUBLISHING COMPANY.
1873.

CONTENTS.

TO THE MEMORY
OF
The friends of my Childhood,
WHOSE ACTS IT HAS GIVEN ME SUCH INFINITE PLEASURE TO
RECORD,
This Little Volume is Reverently Dedicated

BY THE AUTHOR.

PREFACE.

The following story, originally written for the LANCASTER INQUIRER, is founded on facts that came within the personal knowledge of the writer. The characters described are all real ones, as will be attested by many of the older inhabitants, yet living in the region of country where the events described occurred. Belonging to a generation of people and a condition of society that are rapidly passing away, they cannot fail to excite an interest in the minds of those who, living under totally different influences, learn of them only through others. The narrative of John and Mary, or rather of Mary and her child, is founded strictly on facts, and resulted from a state of society that has passed away forever. Whatever faithfully describes the influences and results of the institution of slavery, must become more and more interesting to the present generation, and in the hope that this little volume will in a measure meet this growing want, the writer has consented to its publication in the present form. That some pleasure and profit may result to the reader from its perusal is the earnest desire of

THE AUTHOR.

JOHN AND MARY, THE FUGITIVE SLAVES.

CHAPTER I.
THE OCTORARA.

"Stream of my fathers! sweetly still
The sunset rays thy valleys fill;
Pour slantwise down the long defile,
Wave, wood and spire beneath them smile."

SKIRTING the south-eastern border of Lancaster, county, Pennsylvania, where it forms the dividing line between that and Chester county, is the Octorara creek. It is a beautiful and romantic stream, and after the union of its eastern and western branches, attains considerable size. Along its banks can be found almost every variety of scenery; and every description of romantic and picturesque beauty. The stream itself is a study for the lover of Nature, who would never tire in contemplating it. Now it spreads out a broad bright sheet of glassy surface, glowing like burnished silver, as it reflects the rays of the setting sun, or glistens beneath the full moon's rich flood of glorious light; while slowly, silently and almost imperceptibly it moves forward. Again, it rushes madly down some deep ravine, leaping wildly from rock to rock and dashing its white foam in every direction, as though it bore a message whose supreme importance Nature herself had recognized. Sometimes it traverses a deep forest, where for miles the mighty oak and the kingly pine, with their broad-spreading branches intertwined, almost shut out the light of day; while the whispered murmur of the waters seems like the sigh of some hopeless spirit wafted from the darkness of the unknown.

Again emerging, it threads some green meadow, reflecting the blue heavens above, and the wild flowers and beautiful verdure that skirt its borders. Here and there is a mill-dam that turns the machinery that grinds the grain for the neighboring farmers; while over its breast glides a broad sheet of water, which, falling some distance, forms a miniature Niagara, whose roar can be heard for miles away in the stillness of the night or early morning, and whose voice reaches far and wide when the usually placid stream swells into an angry flood.

One cannot but remark the partiality always felt toward a stream of water by those who dwell upon its borders. Nothing furnishes such solace for their leisure hours as a stroll along its banks. For them it has some ever-present attraction, which retains its freshness as long as life endures.

Forty years ago or more, the period at which our story commences, the Octorara, or that part of it between the junction of the two branches and the Maryland line, was wilder and more romantic than at the present day. The deep, unbroken forests that then lined its banks have been partly cleared away. Houses have been erected where there was undisturbed solitude, lands cleared and cultivated and waterpower made available where then no sound of industry disturbed the stillness of nature.

Still, at that time, it was by no means an unsettled section of country. Public highways leading north and south crossed the stream at intervals, which was passable for all kinds of vehicles at any of the fords, except when swollen by rains or rendered impassable by ice, which was often the case during the winter season.

Much of the land along this stream was even then noted for its fertility, and though farming was laborious, owing to the land being rugged and hilly, it yielded a fair return to industry and skill.

If our readers will glance at a map of Lancaster County they will see, in the southern part of Little Britain Township, a ford of the Octorara marked as "People's ford," possibly from someone of that name having once dwelt there. At the time of which we speak, it was called "Brown's ford," and a family of that name resided there.

As the surroundings of this place will be of some interest to us in the progress of our story, we shall proceed to give a brief description of them.

The road, crossing at this ford, led north and south, and was mainly used, besides neighborhood traveling, by persons hauling lime from Quarryville and vicinity, to points farther south; some to parts of Chester county, and others to Cecil county, Maryland, which was but a few miles distant. The ford was safe and easily crossed when the creek was low, but dangerous when it was swollen.

Indeed, legends prevailed of men and women, who, too venturesome, had attempted crossing at such times and been swept away in the devouring flood. We cannot verify these stories, but do not doubt their accuracy.

The southern bank of the stream at this place, both above and below the ford, was crowned with high hills, covered with a thick undergrowth of dogwood, honeysuckle, and laurel, while high above these towered almost every variety of oak, pine and other forest trees. Here, during the spring time, were myriads upon myriads of feathered songsters, who sought these forest-crowned hills to build their nests and rear their young, and from earliest dawn to dewy eve, they mingled their sweet warblings with the gentle murmurings of the stream below.

Just above the ford, on the southern side, a little brook entered the creek. It had its source some half-mile away, in a south-easterly direction. Along its eastern bank, for some three or four hundred yards from where it mingled its waters with the larger stream, arose a mighty hill, covered with laurel and crowned with majestic oaks. This was called "Laurel hill," and when in bloom, in early summer, was such a picture of beauty as the human eye seldom rests upon.

Three-fourths of a mile below was another crossing, known as "Carter's," where a bridge has since been erected. This was reached from the place we have been describing by a rough and narrow road, which, branching from the main one some 50 yards from the creek, threaded a dark wood for nearly half the distance, ascended a steep hill, and descending a similar one reached Carter's mill just at its foot and close by the ford.

The dwelling in which the Browns of Brown's fording resided was situated about 50 yards from the creek, and exactly at the point where the road to Carter's ford branched off from the main road leading south. It consisted of a one-and-a-half story log house, built at an early period of the settlement of the country, and a brick end which had been added by the proprietor. The lower story of the log end constituted the kitchen, which was ample, after the fashion of the olden time, and contained among other things the old-fashioned "kitchen dresser" on whose open shelves the pewter plates and spoons glistened with repeated scourings; the "knife box" hanging against the wall beneath the lower shelf, where knives and forks were all carefully deposited after being as carefully washed and scoured, while all around the room were hung various kinds of bags and boxes containing things for present and future use. There stands the old-fashioned fire-place, up whose mighty throat the great fire roared and crackled with a consumption of fuel that would never be tolerated at the present day. Just as you enter the kitchen you can see to the right a door which, opening, discloses a flight of steps descending into the cellar, which is large and deep. Above the kitchen are two sleeping rooms and above these a garret of the real old-fashioned pattern. In the other end, if we should pass in, we could see a good sized parlor, without carpet of any description, but with an oaken floor scoured as white as soap and pewter sand would make it; a half-dozen windsor chairs, two arm-chairs, a couple of tables, a Yankee clock, one looking-glass and a fire-place much less than the one we have just examined. Over the parlor are two sleeping rooms, while a flight of stairs leads both to them and a room in the other end.

Leaving the house we cross the main road leading by the door, and look at the log shop where the Browns carry on wagon-making. This is a small building with a ground floor. In front is a large sycamore tree which gives ample shade when shade is needed, while behind it is a magnificent maple in whose thick foliage many a merry bird has built her nest and brought forth her young unharmed.

Just below the shop, and at the base of "Laurel hill," is the spring-house, to which a well-kown path leads, for there is the spring, which never failing in summer's heat or winter's cold, furnishes a supply of as pure, sweet water as ever quenched human thirst.

Up the main road from the house stands the barn, some 75 yards away; it is a small frame building, with one threshing floor, and scarcely sufficient room to store away the products of the small farm. If you look carefully you will see a pair of flails, hanging up in the corner, that are used for threshing; machines for that purpose being unknown in that section in those days. The two pieces of wood which compose each one are tied together with dried eel-skin, that being considered the very best article for the purpose that can be obtained.

Leaving the barn and wandering to the top of the hill in front of it, we see the orchard--apple and peach. It is early autumn and but few peaches are left, but the wealth of the rich, beautiful apples as they cluster on the heavily-laden boughs, form a picture of beauty such as seldom meets the eye.

Looking beyond you can see in the distance glimpses of the "pine barrens," and of these we will now speak.

To the south, south-east and south-west of Brown's ford, beginning but little more than a mile away, lay thousands and thousands of acres of land, to which no one at that time possessed a title. The land was mostly grown up with pine and scrub-oak, or black jack, and in summer time was used as pasture land for the cattle of many small farmers who lived near. At such times it would be dotted over with small herds of cattle, one in each herd wearing a bell, the sound of which was well-known to the owner or his boys, who went out to hunt them if they did not return at the proper time. This they mostly did, and as the summer sun approached the western horizon you could see numerous small herds of cattle, each led by the "bell cow," wending their way quietly toward their homes.

Here and there all through this wilderness stood the log hut of a negro, and sometimes of a white man, built of pine logs and covered with boards or slabs of the same material. Hard by was a small lot or clearing, fenced in and used for a garden. The occupants of these huts picked up a subsistence by working by the day for farmers in Lancaster, Chester and Cecil counties; and sometimes in winter by chopping wood, threshing with the flail, dressing flax and other pursuits of a similar character.

In autumn the people who lived in the vicinity of the barrens appropriated a day or two to hunting up and hauling home pine knots for winter use. These pine knots were the hearts of pine trees that had fallen and the outside decayed, leaving the heart or knot, which was very inflammable and burned for a long time, producing a fine light.

All through the barrens these could be found, sometimes in great quantities together, and when taken home and properly prepared by being split up, they served as kindling and as a means of giving light during the long winter evenings. Placed on the kitchen fire in the wide, old-fashioned fire-place, a good sized pine knot would give all the light that was needed in the room. The old folks could read the papers, the girls wash dishes or spin, and the children learn their lessons by this light without difficulty.

But our readers have not yet been introduced to any of the characters of our story. That pleasure we reserve for our next chapter.

CHAPTER II.
THE BROWNS AND THEIR NEIGHBORS.

"Time rolls his ceaseless flight. The race of yore,
Who danced our infancy upon their knee
And told our wondering boyhood legend's store;
How are they blotted from the things that be!"

THE Brown family, who resided in the house we have described at the ford, consisted at the time of the commencement of our story, of six persons: the father and mother, three children, and a young man about 18 years of age, named Samuel Weaver, an apprentice to the wagon-making business. The father, William Brown, or as he was familiarly known among his neighbors, "Billy Brown," was about 42 years of age, and the two elder children were his by a former marriage. Their mother, after a few brief years of married life, had passed away, and been quietly and sorrowfully laid in the grave-yard at the Friends' Meeting-house, a few miles distant. The elder child, a girl, was some 18 years of age and bore a strong resemblance to her father; her name was Martha. Her brother, named Henry, was two year her junior, and, the neighbors said, favored his deceased mother. Margaret Brown, the present wife of William, was some years his junior, and at the time of which we speak was probably about 35 years of age. Her only child, a boy of six or seven years, named Frank, made up the sixth and last member of the family.

William, or "Billy Brown," as we shall sometimes hereafter call him, was one of those remarkable men, physically, who seem to belong to a past age. He was about six feet high, lacking probably half an inch, and, without an ounce of superfluous flesh, weighing 190 pounds. His shoulders were broad, and rounded very slightly, his chest deep and ample, and his limbs muscular and well formed. He seemed born to accomplish whatever was (physically) within the bounds of possibility.

His ancestors had come over from England with William Penn, at the first Quaker settlement at Philadelphia, and every branch of the family's descendants had retained their connection with that sect.

But to look at "Billy," without taking note of his apparel, one would scarcely put him down as belonging to that staid and quiet society. His small gray eyes, deep-set in his head, had about them a fun-loving twinkle which told that merriment, and even hilarity, were in no way repulsive to his feelings; while his curly black hair, which fell in glossy ringlets over the straight, stiff collar of his Quaker coat, was a reminder that nature had not designed him to live in a world whose only color was drab.

Looking at his head with its high though not broad forehead, its well developed coronal region, its strongly marked perceptive faculties and ample breadth behind the ears, a phrenologist would say that firmness, conscientiousness and courage were his leading characteristics; and that though having a fair and practical intellect, which culture would have developed into a commanding one, he lacked the command of words necessary to convey his ideas with ease or fluency; while those who had the best opportunity to know him, and were capable of judging, would have confirmed this opinion.

A year and more after the death of his first wife, Billy Brown had, in pursuit of his calling, went some six or seven miles up the Octorara to look at some rare and valuable timber on the premises of his friend Joe Simmons, who had sent him word that he had such an article for sale.

Joe was a bachelor, who owned a large tract of land, given him by his father, a small portion of which was farm land, and the remainder covered with heavy timber. When Billy arrived, after looking at the timber he was invited to the house to take dinner, as was the hospitable custom in those days when it was at or near that hour.

Now it was Joe's good fortune to have a housekeeper, whom his father had raised and whom he had known from childhood, amply capable of performing all the duties pertaining to that position, besides being a woman that was in every respect calculated to make home pleasant and comfortable. So at least thought Joe, and events proved that his guest strongly inclined to the same opinion, for he soon returned to visit again the hospitable mansion of his friend, and in a little more than a year, at the quiet and unpretending meeting-house in the neighborhood, where Friends met for divine worship, William Brown and Margaret Lincoln were made man and wife.

Everybody said it was a good match. The Friends, in their quiet way, congratulated each other that both these worthy members had married in the society, and according to their prescribed forms. Joe Simmons was perhaps the only dissatisfied person in the neighborhood, and he only because he had lost his housekeeper.

Margaret Lincoln was the daughter of Scotch Presbyterians, who had emigrated to America just after the close of the Revolutionary war, and settled near Elkton, Cecil county, Maryland. They both died about the year 1800, leaving a family of small children without any means of support.

It was Margaret's good fortune to be "bound out," as the custom then was, to a member of the Society of Friends, residing in Chester county, Pennsylvania, near the Maryland line, named Abraham Simmons. She was kindly used in this family and ever retained for them a grateful remembrance. Naturally of a devotional nature, and attending the meetings of no religious society but the Friends, she soon became attached to their doctrine and principles, and at the age of eighteen made application for admission to membership; this, after careful examination by a committee appointed by the society, was promptly granted. She remained through life one of its most active and devoted members.

When Margaret attained the age of twenty-one, Abraham Simmons made a present to his son Joe of a tract of land on the Octorara, and asked Margaret if she would keep house for him. She consented, and remained there until she met with William Brown, as before mentioned.

At the time we introduced our readers to the Brown family, she was about 35 years of age, and had been married about eight years. Looking at her then, one could hardly imagine a more perfect picture of matured, womanly beauty. Her form was somewhat stout but not unpleasant to look upon. Her heavy tresses of dark-brown hair were drawn back from a forehead smooth as polished marble and almost as white. Her soft hazel eyes looked out upon the world as though it were something to love and make happy; and her nose, slightly Roman, detracted nothing from her beauty, while marking her character as one of ample force.

Her cheeks rivaled the fairest rose in their pure and delicate color, and her mouth and chin, while bearing marks of firmness and decision, did not in any way detract from the uniformity and proportion of her face. The expression of her countenance was genial and benevolent, and one could not look upon her without being most favorably impressed with her appearance.

Such were the Browns, of Brown's ford, in or about the year 1830. Let us now learn something of their neighbors.

A large majority of persons residing in the immediate neighborhood were members of the Society of Friends, and those who inclined that way. They met for public worship at Eastland Meeting-house, some two miles from the ford, on the northern or Lancaster county side. The regular meetings of the society were held on the first and fourth days of the week, those on First day, or Sunday, being generally well attended. When it happened, as was not unfrequently the case, that a "traveling Friend" came round, the gatherings were quite large, the little meeting-house not always being large enough to hold them.

Among the prominent and influential members of the society, who gathered twice a week, in sunshine and storm, in summer's heat and winter's cold, to worship God in their quiet and unpretending way, was Samuel Carter, or "Grandfather Carter" as he was generally called. He resided at Carter's mill, on the Octorara, a short distance below Brown's. as we have already described. He was a widower, with a large family of well-grown up and married children, and was about 75 years of age. He was noted the whole neighborhood over for his great strength of character, his strong sense of justice, indomitable pluck and practical good sense.

Whenever any unusually difficult undertaking was to be accomplished, Grandfather Carter, above all others, was the man to be consulted. His strong common sense and originality often suggested a simple and practical solution of important questions that had long been a puzzle to his less discerning neighbors.

Up the main road leading south from the ford at Brown's, and not more than a mile away, on the very verge of the "Barrens," lived Peggy Keys and her husband Tommy. Peggy was ones of those strong-minded ladies who believed in woman's rights, and what was better, maintained them. Instead of vainly pleading for her rights, as do her less sagacious sisters of modern times, she had started business at the head of the firm and with indomitable pluck maintained her position there. Tommy was a man of some character and by no means a cypher; but he was not captain in that company. He had taken the position of first lieutenant at the beginning, and was in no danger of promotion except from the death of his superior officer.

They owned a reasonably comfortable house and a few acres of land, which they farmed very nicely, Peggy assisting in the out-door work.

She could hoe corn and potatoes, dress flax, rake hay and wheat, and husk corn, as well as men generally. What she could not do herself, she would oversee others in doing; and in that she manifested much ability. Nor was she content to work only at home. When not busy there she would hunt for a job among neighboring farmers, leaving to her two daughters the business of taking care of things at home.

As a corn-husker Peggy was peerless. In the fall of the year she would look out for all the husking that could be secured, and as soon as the grain was dry enough, at it she and Tommy would go. At the first dawn of morning, no matter how cold, she could be seen, with a night-cap or two, and a close-fitting bonnet in addition on her head, to keep out the cold, a heavy tow apron or bib on, and a long, smooth husking peg, made of the best and hardest of hickory, fastened to her hand by a leather strap or eel-skin.

From early dawn to dewy eve these two would toil, stopping only when the welcome dinner-horn called them to their mid-day meal. That meal over Peggy would light her pipe, Tommy would bite off a mouthful of his heavy plug tobacco, and away they would go to their labor, which darkness alone brought to a close. Nor would that always end their toil. Sometimes when there was moonlight, Peggy would direct Tommy to accompany her to the field after supper, and the two would toil till late bed-time at their task.

Nor was this all. No two men in the neighborhood could do more or better work, of this kind, in the same time, than Peggy Keys and her husband.

The bargains were always made by her, and the settlements also. She was captain of that company and maintained her rank in its entirety.

In many respects she was an estimable woman, and under other circumstances might have been extensively useful. She had an active mind but no culture, and as such people mostly are, was an adept in hunting up neighborhood news. Without meaning to do any harm in this way, she often, through want of thought, was the means of making mischief.

Her family had been Quakers, but when she married Tommy, who was not a member, she was disowned. Nevertheless she always attended meeting when a "strange Friend" came along, of which notice was mostly given her. On such occasions she would direct Tommy to yoke the oxen to the cart, that being the only vehicle they were in possession of, and placing a rush-bottom chair in it, he seated on the front part of the cart, they would drive to meeting.

Far over in the "Barrens," some two miles away, at the foot of Goat-hill (so called from there often being goats seen browsing on its summit), lived a colored man who was known throughout the country round by the name of Neddy Johnson. Neddy had been a slave under the law of Pennsylvania, the property of some one in the southern part of Lancaster county. He had been married in early life, but his wife had died, leaving him a boy who went by the name of "Bill." After a short experience in single blessedness, Neddy had married again, joining, his fortunes with a widow named "Till" or "Tilly," who had two worthless boys, now grown to men, known as "Dave" and "Ben." Neddy and his spouse had sought the "Barrens," where they had erected a log cabin, fenced in a small lot, and proposed to make that place their home for the remainder of their days.

Neddy was in many respects a remarkable man. His physical development was grand. He was six feet in height, as straight as an arrow, and weighed about 180 pounds. His strength was most remarkable. Logs of wood that ordinary men could not lift, he could toss into a wagon or cart without an effort. It was said, on what seemed to be good authority, that he had cut, with a cradle, ten acres of well-grown wheat in a day. If any of the farmers wanted a big day's work done, they sent for Neddy. He seemed to work without an effort. Harvest time, though, was his glory. Always leading the mowers or reapers, he walked at their head like a king. No one in all that country was vain enough to believe he was able to "crowd" Neddy at such a time. At threshing with a flail, as was then the custom, he had no peer. It was said he could thresh twenty bushels of wheat in that way in a day; while ten was considered a good day's work for most men.

He had a great deal of native shrewdness and cunning, and withal was perfectly honest and upright.

Neddy possessed in a remarkable degree that peculiar faculty, which in human beings is supposed to represent what in animals is called instinct; but which in the former is possibly the result of very acute and well-trained perceptive powers. If anything was lost and a party started out to find it, Neddy being with them, he was sure to be the lucky one. Often he would go straight to the spot without an apparent effort or thought. If he went fishing the fish were sure to bite at his hook. His traps were the ones the game delighted to enter, and when he went out to shoot pigeons or squirrels, they were sure to present themselves at a convenient place in order to fall before his unerring aim.

Such was Neddy Johnson. Our readers shall know him better in the future.

CHAPTER III.
THE FRIENDS.

"We bring no ghastly halocaust,
We pile no graven stone;
He serves thee best who loveth most
His brother, and thy own."

IT has been already stated, in a preceding chapter, that a large majority of those who resided in the neighborhood of which we have been speaking, were members of the Society of Friends. Indeed the settlement of Friends, of which this formed a part, embraced portions of Lancaster and Chester counties, in Pennsylvania, and Cecil and Harford counties, in Maryland.

Within reach of Brown's ford, by an easy half-day's journey, were not less than six Friends' meeting houses, three of them in Lancaster, two in Cecil and one in Harford county.

These were all embraced within the limits of one quarterly meeting-- Nottingham--which was held alternately at Little Britain, Deer Creek and Brick Meeting-house.

The membership of this was quite large, and embraced many substantial and well-to-do citizens. As a natural consequence the principles, doctrines and customs of Friends had an extensive influence in this section, even among those who but seldom attended their meetings. The leading members were noted for their force of character and self-reliance, and these qualities contributed largely to impress their principles and modes of thought on those who possessed them in a less degree.

In those days the members of that society were much more exacting than at the present time. Music was forbidden in their families, and dancing was a sin scarcely to be atoned for. Any appearance of gayety in dress was frowned down as a sin that should receive no quarter. The elderly Friends wore their clothes of the plainest cut and color, and while to the younger members were allowed some latitude in this respect, there were certain bounds beyond which they were not permitted to go. The young men were permitted to wear coats of soft brown or dark color; but they did not give to the elderly members that supreme satisfaction they enjoyed at seeing a youthful Friend clad in drab. Any color, however, could be tolerated sooner than blue. That was not to be permitted or thought of. The devil never hated holy water with half the unction that a devoted follower of George Fox, at that day, hated a blue coat, especially if it was adorned with gilt or brass buttons--then it was fit only to be deposited in the very inner sanctuary of the Evil One.

A devoted and pious Friend, whose well-tilled acres bordered on the meeting-house at Eastland, had two bright-eyed daughters who had come to that age when unsatisfied yearnings take the place of girlhood's romp and gayety. Regular in their attendance at meeting, as was the imperative law in their domestic circle, they had attracted the attention and excited the admiration of a young man, himself a member of the society, but who had so far departed from established custom as to wear a blue coat. Once or twice he visited the Friend's house to spend an hour or two in company with the girls, and the father bore it with becoming resignation. Patience at last, however, ceased to be a virtue; he said: "Franklin, thee's not wanted here, thee's not wanted, thee may go." The young man looked up in astonishment, but the Friend continued: "I know what thee comes for, but thy coats 's too blue--I tell thee thy coat's too blue." Franklin departed.

More than a quarter of a century since, both the rigid Quaker and the blue-coated youth crossed over the dark river, and all that remained of them on earth was laid peacefully away in the little graveyard near by. In the house, not made with hands, to which they have gone, the angels wear neither blue nor drab, but vestments radiant with the love that embraces within its limits all created beings.

The Friends were noted for their thriftiness. A general supervision was exercised by the officers of the society over the business relations of the members, and at their monthly meetings one of the queries answered by the overseers was: "Are Friends careful to live within the bounds of their circumstances?" Any marked deviation from this received the immediate attention of the officials, and indeed, a member who regarded his standing in the society, was careful to guard against much outward show.

The general restraint upon any inclination toward extravagance, and the industrious and frugal habits of this people, had a tendency to cultivate and encourage a fondness for gain; and the members of the society were proverbial for their "love of money." There were few really poor people among them, though such as were so, were carefully cared for by the meeting.

The quiet ways of the Friends, and their habits of self-restraint developed in them a kind of slyness that peculiarly fitted them, sharpened as it was by a love of money, to make a successful and profitable bargain. Indeed, it was sometimes said, that some prominent Friends were better "dealers" than strict honesty or the pure spirit of Christianity would warrant.

A drover in a neighboring village had bought some fat cattle from a farmer who was a member of the Presbyterian church. They were sold by live weight, and when weighed a few days afterward they had lost many pounds. The drover complained bitterly, and charged that they had been fed salt and allowed to drink a large quantity of water, in order to increase their weight. In the presence of several persons who were at the village store, in the evening, he said:

"Prispiterans will do that, they'll allus git their steers to drink all they kin. Feed 'em all the salt they'll eat. I know 'em, av bin fooled with 'em afore."

"How is it with the Quakers, Abe," said a sly fellow in the crowd, who perceived several members of that society present, "will they do so too?"

"Yes," said Abe, too indignant to conceal the truth, "some of 'em will; the strict un's will."

The remark was greeted with a hearty laugh, in which all parties joined.

The Friends were noted for their hospitality. The belated traveler never asked in vain for a night's lodging.

"The long-remembered beggar was their guest,
Whose beard descending, swept his aged breast"

No one turned away empty handed from their dwellings who was needy or in want; though they were the last people to encourage idleness or unthrift.

25

Their social disposition was also manifested by the frequent interchange of visits with each other. These took place mostly on First-day afternoons, as the rest of the week was generally taken up with labor, and they did not observe the Sabbath as strictly as some other sects.

Their quarterly meeting days, however, were the great occasions for the manifestation of social hospitality. To these meetings there was generally a large turnout, not only the members, but many others within reach attending them. Those near the place, and within easy distance of it, made ample provision for the reception of guests, and gave them a genuine old-fashioned welcome. The meeting sometimes lasted until late in the afternoon, when "weighty" Friends were present who had much to communicate, and at such times those from a distance had to remain in the neighborhood until the next day. It often happened that beds had to be made up for the family, on the floor of the parlor and kitchen, their ordinary sleeping accommodations not being sufficient for all the strangers. But with all these disadvantages, the entertainments of Friends, at these meetings, were such as to leave always a pleasant and kindly remembrance. Roast beef, veal, and chickens young and fat, graced the well-filled table. Butter, golden and sweet as the scent of new-mown hay, bread, white as snow itself, and pies, and puddings to which no words can do justice, added their attractions. Sociability as genuine and natural as the blush which often mantled the cheeks of the pretty Quaker girls, pervaded the household, and the habitual restraint that generally rested upon the members was for a time removed.

But there was one Friend within the limits of this quarterly meeting, always regular in his attendance, whom neither the attractions of hospitality, the charms of companionship, nor the inconvenience of an empty stomach, could ever tempt to take a meal at the house of an acquaintance on his way to or from meeting. This was John Brown, a brother of Billy's, who dwelt on the borders of the "Barrens," in Cecil County, a short distance from the Pennsylvania line. Mounted on his little sorrel horse, with a saddle and bridle as plain and unpretending as ingenuity could possibly make them, dressed in a drab coat of the most rigid color and pattern, and a hat whose broad brim was a passport to the good graces of the strictest Friend, he would jog off to meeting, ten or fifteen miles away, as the case may be, and return without ever accepting an invitation to partake of refreshments.

Unlike his brother, he seemed adapted by nature for one of the strictest of the sect. In early life, when in attendance at Friends' meeting, he had been visited by the "Spirit," his whole body shaking violently for some minutes, and it seemed as though there had been a marked change in his character ever afterward. Genial and hospitable at home, he accepted no invitation to visit abroad, except under the most pressing circumstances. Twice a week he repaired to the little brick meeting-house at West Nottingham, a mile or two to the south, where Friends met to worship, and permitted no considerations of business or weather to deter him.

The membership here was small, sometimes but two or three being in attendance; but among them always was John Brown. On one occasion, it is said that none were present but himself; but John entered the house, took his usual seat, which he occupied the allotted time, and then retiring, wended his way to his humble home.

Poor fellow, his faithful head was long since laid beneath the sods of Nottingham graveyard and sedge-grass and wild briar for years have bloomed about his humble grave; but those who knew and understood him well cherish no kinder or more tender memory than that of the plain, honest Quaker--John Brown.

The secret of his unwillingness to stop at the houses of Friends and partake of their hospitality, is thus explained: Deeply devoted to the doctrine and principles of the society, he was specially so to the testimony, which they bore against negro slavery. Though living in a slave State, and surrounded by influences hostile to the development of an anti-slavery sentiment, he had resolved that so far as he was concerned the testimony of the society against that institution should be maintained in its purity. In pursuance of this, he would neither taste, touch or handle, when it was practicable to avoid it, anything that was the product of slave labor. The clothes he wore were all of home manufacture, and the sugar, coffee and other articles consumed by him were the products of free labor, at least were represented as such to him. When away from home he did not care to make this fact known, and consequently thought it the best way to avoid stopping where he would be liable to make use, inadvertently, of slave-grown produce.

In fact, the opposition of Friends, passive though it generally was, to the system of slavery, had much to do with preventing the growth of a bitter pro-slavery sentiment. Their early and faithful testimony against this wrong had made an impression on the outside world, and, though the section of country of which we have been speaking was not anti-slavery, it was surely much less pro-slavery than it otherwise would have been. True, there was a bitter prejudice against the negro, and a general conviction that he was better off in slavery than in freedom, if he had a "good master," but it was believed that there were many bad masters, and a great deal of wrong done to slaves. The presence of the weary and stricken fugitive always brought out a sentiment favorable to his protection, and but few could be found hardy enough to openly advocate the return of one to bondage.

The houses of Friends were generally the places for runaway slaves to resort to. They were here doubly secure both on account of the known opposition of that people to slavery, and the quiet tact with which they managed affairs of the kind that were committed to their care.

At about the period of which we have been speaking, there arose a dissension in the Society, which terminated in an open rupture and a division into two separate organizations, each claiming to be the original Society, then and now known as Orthodox and Hicksite. History teaches that there are no disputes so bitter and unreasonable as those of a theological character, and this one was no exception to the rule. Our quiet little community in the vicinity of Brown's ford was profoundly agitated by it, and arrayed themselves into two hostile sections, as bitter and uncompromising as sectarian bigotry could make them. It seemed as though the very milk of human kindness was turned to gall by this unhappy feud, that rent in twain those who ever should have been united in the bonds of love.

Billy and Margaret Brown, with Grandfather Carter and his family, espoused the side of those known as Hicksites, who were indeed greatly in the majority in that settlement. But the other side made up in zeal and activity what they lacked in numbers, and proceeded to "disown" all of the opposite party. This proceeding led to frequent personal interviews, between the parties, which were marked by anything but kindness and good feeling.

Among the leaders of those known as Orthodox Friends was one, living some three miles from the ford, on the Lancaster county side, known by the name of Jos. Bailey. He had manifested great bitterness toward the Hicksite Friends, and was cordially disliked by them; but as our readers will become better acquainted with him in the progress of this story, we shall say nothing further of him at present.

CHAPTER IV.
A VISITOR.

"In faith and hope the world will disagree,
But all mankind's concern is charity;
All must be false who thwart this one great end;
And all of God, that bless mankind, or mend."

IT was early in the forenoon of a beautiful autumn day. The woods around Brown's ford were just beginning to clothe themselves in the gorgeous drapery of the season. Up the little brook, that entered the creek near the ford, the maples were tinged with crimson, which contrasted finely with the deep green of the laurel and the yet unfaded freshness of the oak. Along the banks of the creek the gum and birch showed traces of the frost king in their red and yellow leaves; while high up on the hill the hickories waved their fading verdure in the soft autumn air. The squirrels were busy gathering their winter stores, and as they leaped from branch to branch, or from tree to tree, now and then a leaf would be severed from its hold, and floating, dancing, eddying through the dreamy atmosphere, would settle down at length on its last resting-place--the earth.

Billy Brown was busily at work in his shop, seated at the "wheel pit" near the door, mortising hubs for wagon-wheels. Early in the morning the air had been chilly, and a fire was necessary, but it had gone down and the embers smouldered on the hearth. On the floor sat Frank, building imaginary houses from blocks gathered up about the shop. Near him lay "Ring," the great house dog, so called from a white ring around his neck, though otherwise he was as black as nature well could make him. He was a faithful dog, Ring was, and followed Frank wherever he went, up and down the creek, through the laurel hill, or out to the barrens in search of the cows, and was only tempted to leave him when some very attractive game crossed his path.

The sun shone forth with all the soft brilliancy peculiar to the season. The gentle music of the Octorara, as it stole softly by, fell dreamily on the ear. From the meadow, on its opposite bank, could be heard the shrill "bob-white" of the partridge, while from the wood on the hill came the less musical bark of the squirrel.

In the barn, Neddy was at work threshing out the summer's crop, and the dull, regular sound of the flail re-echoed through the neighboring woods. From a wood nearly a mile away resounded the axes of the "boys," who had that morning gone out to cut the winter's firewood.

"Father, there comes a stranger! there comes a stranger!" said Frank suddenly, as a man, riding from the direction of Carter's mill, stopped at the fence near the shop and was hitching his horse; "it's old Josey Bailey, he's comin' to have another meetin'," said he, as the man approached the shop.

"Hush! hush!" said his father in an undertone, "keep quiet."

The man who was thus approaching has already been made known to our readers as a leading member of the Orthodox Friends. The boy's remarks had reference to the frequent interviews between the two parties, while the Orthodox were engaged in "disowning" the Hicksites.

"Well, Billy," said he as he approached the shop and stood in front of the open door.

Billy Brown looked up from his work, glanced inquiringly at the stranger, said "well Josey," and in a moment was as busy as ever with mallet and chisel.

The visitor leaned against the side of the doorway, hesitated a minute or two, and then began: "Is thee in want of any help just now, Billy?"

"No, I guess not," was the quiet reply; while a still greater degree of curiosity flitted across his countenance.

"No threshing to do?" asked Josey in the same quiet tone.

"No," was the reply, "Neddy is doing the threshing."

"No wood to cut?" persisted the inquirer.

"No, the boys are cutting the winter's wood," was answered.

"Nor corn to husk?"

"No, Peggy Keys is to husk the corn, I always give her that job."

"Don't Margaret need any help, either?" persisted Josey, without the least symptoms of disappointment at the negative answers returned to all his inquiries.

"No, I guess not. Martha came home from Westtown last week, and she don't need any other help."

Friend Bailey in the meantime looked as calm as a summer's morning. He knew that his visit would not be a failure, though all his preliminary questions had been answered negatively. He felt confident of success when the main question would come fairly up.

Seating himself on a large block, close by the door-sill, and looking quietly around, he said:

"Davy was over to see me last night, and he expects some folks along in a few days, and would like to have a place for them a little while."

This was said in a low, earnest tone, and the remark seemed at once to have the desired effect. Billy Brown's interest in the matter was now fully aroused. He laid his mallet on the side of the wheel-pit, and looking up earnestly into the face of the questioner said:

"How many are there?"

"Only two, though I believe there is a child with them," was the reply. "It is a man and woman, and their little boy about a year old. I thought this a good place for them to stay until Davy can take them on farther. I called to see Sammy Carter this morning and he thinks this as good a place as we can get. So I came up to see if you could take them."

Billy Brown understood perfectly well that these were fugitive slaves, for whom shelter and a place of concealment was wanted until they could be conveyed to a place of greater safety. With strong and inveterate prejudices against the colored race, he was pre-eminently a just man, and would not knowingly permit a wrong to be done to any one when in his power to prevent it. Besides, the influence of the teaching of Friends made him all the more willing to do what was in his power to assist an escaping fugitive.

"I'll have to see mother about it," he said at length, rising to his feet, "let's go to the house and see what she has to say."

The two then walked slowly toward the house, which was some thirty or forty yards distant.

No one knew better than Billy Brown that asking "mother," as he called his wife, about such a matter as this was a mere form. But it was his way; he never did anything of importance, or entered into any arrangement without first consulting her.

Margaret Brown was busily engaged in ironing, in the large kitchen, when the two entered. "Well, Margaret," said Friend Bailey in his quiet way, "how is thee?" "I'm well; is thee well, Josey?" said she in a tone indicating surprise, while the corners of her mouth showed unusual firmness. She probably thought that he came on business connected with the division.

"Mother," said Billy when they were seated, "Josey has come to see if we could keep some folks for a while that Davy expects to bring along soon. A man and woman and their child. He'll bring them here in a few days."

The firm look about the corners of her mouth vanished, and her eye softened as she said: "Yes, I guess we can; somebody will have to keep them."

"Grandfather Carter and Josey were talking it over this morning, and they thought they had better be brought here," said Billy.

"Yes," remarked the visitor, "this is rather a by-place, and they wouldn't be as likely to look for them here as some other places; besides you have no bad neighbors."

"I think we can keep them," said Margaret, "when will he bring them?"

"As soon as they arrive and rest a little," said Josey; "they will be along in a few days."

33

He then bid farewell and started out. With a look of satisfaction he mounted his horse, turned its head toward the creek, passed over the ford, and ascending the hill beyond was soon lost to sight in the distance.

At half-past eleven o'clock Martha Brown came out on the porch, with the tin dinner-horn, and blew on it loud and long. This she repeated three times, and then feeling sure that the boys and Neddy could not fail to hear it, she returned into the kitchen and bestirred herself to help set the tables and place dinner upon them.

We say "tables," because the Brown family, following the custom of those days in that section, did not eat at the same table with the negroes. Consequently Neddy was always set at a table by himself. He had the same articles of food, was used precisely like the rest in every other particular, but was seated at a table by himself. He had always been used to this, and therefore considered it no degradation.

The boys came in a few minutes before twelve, hungry and tired. Frank was sent to the barn to tell Neddy again to come. When they were all seated at dinner Billy said:

"Neddy, I'm going to have a man to help us. Would thee like to have him help thrash?"

Neddy sometimes stammered, especially when a little excited,

"Wh--who is'e?" said he, a shade of dissatisfaction passing over his face.

"He's from Meraland," was the reply, "one of Davy's men."

"Dey's worth nothin'--ging--god I'se tried 'em," said Neddy, evidently displeased at the idea of having competition in his field of labor, "dey's better off where dey is."

"Come, Neddy," said Margaret, "thee musn't talk that way; the poor creeters have been used very bad I expect."

"Su--sum of 'em is," said he, evidently relenting, "but sum's powerful on'ry. I'se seen a heap of em."

"They'll be here in a day or two," pursued Margaret, and we must take good care of 'em; they won't be here long."

"Yes 'um," said Neddy, evidently softened toward the fugitives by this last remark.

After dinner was over Margaret said: "Neddy, Frank's Guinea hen has stolen her nest somewhere in the Laurel hill; we've all been trying to find it. The boys have hunted for it, and Martha and me have been all over the hill. We hear her cackling there ev'ry day but can't find a bit of it." "Can't thee find it for us?"

"Yes 'um," said Neddy, "guess I might," and away he started toward the hill.

In about ten minutes Neddy came back, his large, honest black face fairly shining with delight; in his old felt hat were ten or twelve Guinea eggs.

"Well, I do say! how is it thee always finds things," said Margaret, "here we've been hunting for that nest for more'n a week, and thee found it in a few minutes."

"Dun no," said Neddy, "I jes' went over dar to de rock fornentz de barn up in de lorrels, and dar's de nest, in under de edge of de rock, hind a little bush."

"Well, I declare! and we were all round that rock. Neddy, thee's a lit le too sharp for the rest of us." Neddy walked off toward the barn a good deal flattered with this remark.

"It seems so queer that Neddy can always find everything," said Margaret, when he was gone.

The evenings were quite cool. As they were seated that evening around the broad kitchen fireplace, on which a bright fire was burning, Margaret said:

"Father, I've just been wondering where we'll put these folks when they come; I guess we'll have to fix up a place in the garret for them."

"Well," said Billy, "I guess that will do very well."

"Yes," was the reply, "Martha and me'll fix it up to-morrow. Frank can help. I wonder when they'll come?"

"In a few days, I reckon. We'll git word afore they come."

Accordingly the next day the garret was "fixed up" for the reception of the strangers. The rubbish which usually accumulates in such a place was removed to the part over the new end of the house, and that over the old end, which was large and roomy, was arranged for them to sleep in. A bedstead, which had been taken apart and laid away, was put up and corded. A bed-tick was taken to the barn and well filled with clean wheat straw, which made a bed good enough for a king. A bolster, pillows and bed clothes were then procured, and the bed was soon ready for the guests.

A little home-made cradle, which had rocked successively all the young Browns in their babyhood, was brought out from among the rubbish and placed beside the bed, for the little one that was expected. This cradle was quite a curiosity in its way, having been made by Billy Brown when such a thing was first needed in the family.

It was made of oak boards, planed off and nailed together; the rockers had been worked into shape with a drawing knife, and fastened to the body with long nails. It was a very rough piece of workmanship, but answered the purpose admirably. When filled with the little straw-cradle-bed and small pillow, and covered with the cradle quilt, it looked quite inviting.

Frank undertook to help Martha and his mother fix up the garret; but finding in one corner of it a half dozen Baer's Almanacs, filled, he said, with "nice picters," and a pile of Village Records that had been lain away there, the services he rendered were not of a very satisfactory character.

When all was done, Margaret said: "Now, Martha, everything is ready for them. They will come here at night and we can just send them to bed without any trouble."

Billy Brown was at work in the shop that day as usual. About the middle of the forenoon Peggy Keys came along.

"Well, Billy," said she, "when'll thee want us to go to work at the corn. Tommy's bin gittin' home pine-knots and wood, and he'll be done this week, and we kin go to work at it next week if thee wants it done; but some people thinks it had better stand a while yet; however, I don't know but what it'll do well enough if there don't a warm spell come, and even if there did thy crib's purty open and it won't be likely to heat."

"You can begin whenever you want to," said Billy, looking up momentarily, and then resuming his work.

"Well, then, I guess we'll try to git at it some time next week," said she; "has thee any fire in the hearth there, Billy?"

"Yes, I guess so, it's most gone out though; I guess there's some there."

Peggy then stepped toward the hearth, took out her pipe and tobacco from her ample pocket, filled the pipe carefully, and picking up a long shaving from the shop floor, proceeded to light it, and then sat down on a large block near by to enjoy a smoke.

After a few minute's silence, during which she puffed diligently away, she said:

"Billy, are the Orthodox and Hicksites a goin' to go together agin?"

"Why?" said Billy, a little startled by the abruptness of the question and not exactly comprehending it.

"Well," said Peggy, now fully enjoying her smoke. "I was at the mill yesterday; we took down a little corn and rye to git ground and I went along to tell 'em how I wanted it done, and while I was there I seen old Josey Bailey ride up, and him and Grandfather Carter had a long talk together and seemed to be very sociable, and then he come up this way. And then in the afternoon I was over at old Sallie Johnson's to git some weavin' done, and while I was there Bella Fulton come there, and she sed she was past here and old Josey was here talkin' to thee and Margaret, and I jest thought that mebby you were tryin to git together agin."

The length of this speech had given Billy ample time to reflect, and he saw clearly that she had come on purpose to find out on what business the Orthodox Friend had been there the day before.

He worked away more busily than ever and said:

"Don't thee think it would be better for us to come together?"

"Yes I do," said she solemnly, as the heavy clouds of smoke rolled upward toward the roof of the shop. "If they can, I think it would be better, but I didn't know whether they were tryin' it or not for certain," said she inquiringly.

These questions were getting troublesome, and he determined to try a flank movement.

Looking up from his work as though he had not heard her last remark, he said: "Peggy, what are you goin' to charge for huskin' corn this year?"

This remark had the desired effect. Peggy's thoughts were at once diverted from their original channel, and blowing out a large volume of smoke, she said, sharply: "Well, I reckon it's wuth as much as it was last year and year afore. We charged five cents a barrel then and nobody grumbled."

"Some people are doin' it for four cents," said Billy, working away with all his might.

"Well, they're welcome to the job if they want it, but they'll not do it like we do. We take off the husks nice and clean, strip off all the silk and tie up the fother in nice little sheaves. Then we shock it up keerfully, and don't leave a husk or a corn-stalk layin' around. Besides, when we meesure the corn we allus shake the barrel three times, and pile as many ears on top as'll lay. Nobody could do it fairer or better'n we do; thee knows that Billy."

Billy did know it, and he had not the slightest notion of getting any one else to husk the corn; but he did not want to be asked any more questions about Friend Bailey's visit.

"Well, Peggy," said he, "we'll not quarrel about the price, if you do the work well; but thee knows corn's very cheap this year, and I want to have it done as cheap as I can. You may go to work at it next week if it suits."

Peggy looked satisfied at this, knocked the ashes from her pipe, deposited it in her pocket, gazed at the creek a few minutes, asked if the boys were "goin' to school this winter," and finally started toward home, saying "farewell" as she passed out of the shop.

As she walked slowly up the road she said to herself, "I wonder what's the reason Billy wouldn't tell me what old Josey was after yesterday. I'll find it out yet some day."

This was Fourth-day, and at half-past ten o'clock Billy and Margaret Brown started to Friends' meeting. After meeting was over, Grandfather Carter came up to Billy and said, quietly: "I seen Davy this morning. The folks have come all safe. He'll bring them to your house to-morrow night."

CHAPTER V.
THE FUGITIVES.

"Our fellow-countrymen in chains!
Slaves in a land of light and law!
Slaves--crouching on the very plains
Where rolled the storm of Freedom's war!"

NIGHT settled down dark and chill in the vicinity of Brown's ford. In the gloaming, heavy clouds were seen scudding across from the eastward, and the low moaning of the wind through the forest betokened an approaching storm. From the tall oaks on Laurel hill great owls sent forth their "who--hoo, who--hoo, who--hoo--e," which was answered by others from the direction of Carter's mill, adding to the gloom and loneliness of the scene.

The family were seated around the broad kitchen fire-place, from which an ample fire, blazing up the great throat of the chimney, sent light and heat throughout the room.

"The owls are makin' a heap of noise to-night," said Billy, looking up from the newspaper which he had been reading, "it's a purty sure sign of a storm. I guess we're going to have the Equinoctial."

"I wonder if them people will come to-night," said Margaret, looking out into the impenetrable gloom; "it's dreadful dark."

"Yes, they'll come. Davy would sooner come a dark night than a light one," was the answer.

"Poor things!" said she, as she leaned against the window, listening to the low murmuring of the wind.

"Did thee chain Ring, Henry?" said his father.

"Yes, I chained him," said Henry, who was busily engaged in making a "pop-gun" for Frank.

Ring was a remarkably quiet and peaceful dog in day-time; but watchful and even savage at night. He seemed to have a marked dislike for colored persons, and, unless it was some one he knew, would not permit one to approach the house even in day-time. For this reason it was thought best to have him chained when Davy and his people were expected.

Whether this disposition of Ring's was a natural prejudice against color; or a vicious habit, learned him in his youth by persons who wanted to frighten "niggers," I am not prepared to say. I am only sure that such was the fact.

The clock in the little parlor rang out the hour of nine, and yet there was no sound of approaching footsteps. Margaret passed out on the porch and listened. The great owls still hooted in the forest and answered each other from hill to hill. The wind, freighted with dampness, had increased in intensity, and shrieked warnings of an approaching storm. With a silent prayer that no harm should come to the poor wanderers, she quietly returned into the house.

"Frank, it's time for him to go to bed," said she, gently, "he is very sleepy."

"No I ain't: I ain't sleepy; look!" said the boy, opening his eyes to their utmost capacity. "My eyes are wide open."

The mother smiled at this rather strained evidence of wakefulness; but he was allowed to remain.

About half-past nine the little yard gate in front of the kitchen door opened and swung too, footsteps were heard on the porch, and a quiet, firm knock against the kitchen door followed. To the response, "come in," the door quietly opened, and a gray-haired mulatto man, slightly made and somewhat stooped, entered; he was followed by a woman some 25 or 30 years old, of middle size, darker in color and carrying a child in her arms.

A man, quite tall, about the same age and color, wearing a high, old-fashioned hat, followed her.

"Why Davy," said Billy, holding out his hand, "thee's got along. It's a purty dark night, ain't it? Thee's brought the folks through. Come up to the fire."

"Yes," said Davy, taking the offered hand, and then moving toward the fire, "we've got along."

Davy was a man of few words.

Margaret had placed chairs for the three near the fire, where they now seated themselves. As they sit there we shall introduce our readers to them more fully.

David McCann, or "Davy," as he was usually called by those who knew him, was a mulatto man, and, at the time of the occurrences we are relating, was, probably, upward of seventy years of age. He lived in an old log house near the Conowingo road, not far from where the line now divides Fulton and Little Britain townships, and about two miles from the Maryland line. The old house, even at that remote period, had a tumble-down appearance, and has since entirely disappeared. It was situated in an open common, with a small lot near by fenced in for a garden.

Here Davy, with his wife Nancy, who followed the business of a midwife, had lived for many years; so long, indeed, that the memory of the oldest inhabitant in that section run not to the contrary.

Tradition had it that he at one time was a slave, that he had been a teamster in the American army during the Revolutionary war, and received his freedom as a reward for faithful and meritorious services. Whether these were facts or not, one thing is undeniable: Davy was a most untiring enemy of slavery, and a safe and almost invariably successful guide for fugitives. The most marvelous tales were told of his achievements in that line. The public mind had settled down into the conviction that a runaway slave, once in his hands, could not be recaptured. Shrewd, quick-witted and cool-headed, with a knowledge of human nature that amounted to genius, he seemed equal to any emergency. It was said that at one time some runaways were concealed in the upper story of the old log house where he lived. Their owners came there in pursuit of them, with the conviction in their minds that they were there. Davy met them at the door and so charmed them with his apparent candor, frankness and innocence, that they left the house without a search, convinced that they had been misinformed in regard to the whereabouts of their slaves.

At another time he was arrested while in Maryland and carried to Elkton, and there placed in the county jail, on charge of assisting in the escape of fugitives. But so carefully had Davy covered up his tracks, that not a jot of evidence could be found against him, though he was confined there for nearly a year.

Looking at him as he sat before the blazing hearth in Brown's kitchen, on that gloomy autumn evening, he was indeed a study. His color was about, as stated in the song of "Dan Tucker," that of a "chaw of terbacker." His head was high, with the organs of firmness and benevolence, well developed, while his forehead, though not ample, was well proportioned and showed a decided predominance of the perceptive or observing faculties. The width of his head above and behind the ears showed that caution, cunning and courage were important and leading elements of his character.

But the most remarkable feature in Davy's appearance was his eyes. They were small, black, restless, deep-sunk in his head, and seemed to have a peculiar fascination about them. When he was sitting quietly they were bright, piercing, and restless; but when excited they fairly blazed with intensity, though in other respects he would seem perfectly cool.

One of his marked peculiarities, and one that always attracted the attention of strangers, was his extravagant use of tobacco. It was rare indeed to see him without a mouthful of that article. He consumed it with great rapidity, his jaws opening and shutting upon it as though they were run by machinery, while he squirted the juice in all directions.

The two who accompanied him on this evening, as our readers have already surmised, were JOHN AND MARY, THE FUGITIVE SLAVES.

John, as we have already stated, was tall and somewhat slender. He was of a dark brown color, and had a peculiarly stolid look. Whether he yearned for freedom, or feared a return to slavery, his appearance gave no indication. As expressionless as the earth he trod upon, his face gave no clue to whether the memories of the past or the hopes of the future stirred the secret recesses of his heart. With his hat in his hand, he sat bolt upright, without the outward manifestations of a single emotion. He was there, he lived, that was all.

Not so with Mary, the woman by his side, who still holds her child upon her knee, where he has sunk into a quiet slumber. Her deep, earnest eye, as it rests upon her sleeping babe, tells eloquently what emotions stir her heart. Her face is a strong one, and in every lineament is depicted an interest that centers in him alone. All the diamonds that glitter in the crowns of the world's proudest rulers; all the luxuries in which the nabobs and princes of the earth are reveling; all the wealth and grandeur that imagination can picture, could not tempt her for one moment from her devotion to that little, homeless, helpless child.

The maternal feeling speaks out in every feature, and sweeps over every other emotion; it would carry her through fire and water, to martyrdom and death, rather than let her part from him.

Margaret Brown gazed at her long and earnestly, and her soft hazel eyes filled with sympathetic tears. Though gentle and kind-hearted, she, too, had a goodly share of prejudice against color. But Mary's tired, weary look conquered her for the time, and she moved softly to her side and said:

"Let me have the little one, thee looks so tired."

"No, missus," was the reply, as she clutched him nervously, "I'll hol' im, I'se not much tired."

But Margaret had won her heart; the woman followed her gratefully with her dark, earnest eyes, her face relaxing some of its intensity, and softening under the influence of unaffected kindness.

"I'll leave these people with you for a little while," said Davy, at length; "I'll take 'em away in a week or two. I 'spect I'll be round a fore long to see you again."

"Won't thee stay all night?" inquired Billy, "it's mighty dark and looks as if it was goin' to rain."

"No, 'twon't rain afore midnight," was the reply, "and I've traveled a heap at night. I'm never afeard."

So Davy arose from his chair, spoke a word or two to John and Mary, said "farewell" to the Browns, and started out into the dark, cheerless, gloomy night.

Billy Brown followed him out, and closed the door.

"Davy." said he, "does thee think anybody's lookin' for these folks?"

"Not that I know of. I 'spect there'll be, though. But I reckon I'll find 'em out afore they git 'em."

"Thee'll let us know, then, I 'spose?"

"Yes, I'll let you know in time."

Davy now started. Billy waited until he was some distance away, when he unchained Ring and let him run at large. He then passed into the house.

Frank had fallen asleep and been carried to bed. The "boys" had retired to their room, and were already snoring. Martha had also gone to bed. Margaret and the fugitives remained.

"Mother," said Billy, as he returned to the kitchen, "I 'spose it's bed-time. Will thee let these people see where they're to go?"

She lighted a tallow-candle and said to Mary: "Come, now, and I'll show thee your bed; then John can find the way up." Mary followed silently up the winding stairs to the garret, where their bed had been prepared. A faint expression of satisfaction passed over her face as she saw the comfortable bed in the cradle for her child, and when the little fellow was undressed and covered up nice and warm, she fairly broke down. "Oh! missus," said she, "de people here's so good;" and leaning her dark face against the bedstead wept long and bitterly.

Margaret waited silently until her emotion subsided, and then pointing to some night-clothes that lay on the chair near the bed, set the candle at the top of the stairs, and said:

"Leave the light here, and when you are in bed I'll come and get it."

She then passed down-stairs, and directed John to go up and leave the light burning till some one came for it. In a few minutes Billy ascended to the garret, and, looking carefully around to see that nothing was on fire, carried the candle back to the kitchen, where Margaret still remained.

It was eleven o'clock, and the family were usually in bed at nine; but still these two lingered, and did not feel like retiring. The occurrences of the evening had made a profound impression, and given them a new experience in real life. They had never harbored fugitive slaves before, and were just beginning to realize both the righteousness of the act and its probable consequences. The weary, homeless creatures in the garret were to them a sacred charge, but they could not forget that this charge brought with it a good deal of possible danger.

They had never seen slave-hunters, but had heard fearful tales of their cruelty, not only to runaways, but to those who harbored and assisted them. They knew but little about the law, but had a vague idea that it punished severely any one who helped away a fugitive slave. It is no wonder, therefore, that a certain feeling of uneasiness crept over them as they thought of these things.

But any one who might have supposed it to be an easy matter to takes these fugitives away by force, would have found himself woefully mistaken. Though Billy Brown was a man who never sought a quarrel, it was not in his nature to shrink from one. He construed the doctrine held by Friends, in relation to turning the other cheek when one was smitten, in a spiritual sense, and had not the slightest faith in its literal application. Besides, he was a powerful man physically, as we have already stated, and would not hesitate to use his utmost efforts in a cause so manifestly just.

"What'll we do, father," said Margaret, inquiringly, after they had been seated for some time, "if they should come here for John and Mary?"

"I don't think they'll come," was the reply.

"Well, but if they do?"

"Well, I guess we'll have to try and keep 'em off. I wouldn't like to see them folks carried back; would thee?"

"No," wearily, "but it's dreadful late. Hadn't we better go to bed. I'll cover the fire."

That done, weary and tired, they sought repose, and were soon wrapped in the quiet embrace of sleep.

CHAPTER VI.
PASSING EVENTS.

----"View them near
At home, where all their worth and power are placed;
And where their hospitable fires burn clear,
And there the lowest farm-house hearth is graced
With manly hearts, in piety sincere."

HENRY BROWN, and Samuel Weaver, the apprentice, awakened before daylight the next morning and found the storm had broken in full fury. The rain poured down in torrents, while the wind shrieked around the building like the wailing of unquiet spirits. They arose, and dressing themselves in the darkness, groped their way to the kitchen. Here they proceeded to make the fire. Drawing forward the live coals which had been covered with ashes, they deposited the latter in an old tin bucket that was used for the purpose; and then proceeded to put the "back-log" in position This was an immense log, usually gnarled or knotty, and was laid at the back of the fire-place, against the wall. The andirons were then put in their places and a much smaller log placed on them; this was called the fore-stick. The space between the back-log and fore-stick was now filled up with smaller wood, and on top of it the coals that had been preserved were placed. Some kindling, that had been brought from the shop the evening before, was then applied, and soon a cheerful fire rewarded their labors.

Henry then took the iron tea-kettle, which was sitting on the dish-bench, filled it with spring water, that had been brought up the evening before, and hung it over the fire to boil. He then lighted a tallow-candle, carried it up to Martha's room door and awakened her, saying it was time to get up.

John and Mary came down at the first appearance of daylight, leaving the little boy still sleeping.

The "old folks," as Margaret and Billy were called by the boys, slept later than usual, and when they appeared breakfast was nearly ready.

The table where Neddy eat when there, was set out for the fugitives, and a plentiful meal placed on it; they eat but little, however, and Mary left the table to go up-stairs for her boy. She soon brought him down and seated him near the fire.

"Neddy'll hardly be here to-day," said Billy, "It's raining too hard. John, I had intended thee to help him thrash; can thee thrash?"

"Yes, sir," said John, mechanically.

"It's too damp to thrash to-day; I guess thee may clean out the stables. Does thee know how to do that?"

"Yes, sir, I dun clean 'em out."

"I'll show thee how we do it; there's not much else for thee to do to-day, it's so wet."

After breakfast Billy accompanied John to the barn and instructed him in the art and mystery of cleaning stables. There was not much to do, and he expected the job would be finished before dinner. He then repaired to the shop, where he and the boys worked industriously till noon.

"What does thee call the little boy, Mary?" said Margaret, after the men had gone from breakfast.

"I calls him Charley, Missus," said she, "dats what de one's name 'at died; I calls dis one de same."

"Is this the only one thee has livin'?"

"No, Missus, I'se got for mor', ges dey's livin', I dunno tho. Dey sol' 'em to Georgi. I'se not seen none uv 'em for dis tree years. Dis one cum since, an' I fetched him away. I clar to God, Missus, it ud kill me if dey'd take dat chile. Fore God, I'd sooner see 'im put in dat fire an' burn to ashes."

Her eye gleamed with a dangerous fire as she said this, and the strong lines of her face stood out with wonderful distinctness. She evidently meant what she said.

Margaret was startled. She was not prepared for such an outburst of passionate earnestness. It was so unlike anything she had been used to, in her intercourse with the quiet and peaceful people of that section, that she thought it must be wicked. At any rate, such a spirit was directly at variance with the teachings of Friends, and felt exceedingly unpleasant to her. But she could not find it in her heart to rebuke the woman, whose wrongs excited her warmest sympathy; so she was silent.

When the family were called to dinner, Billy went to the barn to see how John had progressed with his work. He found he had accomplished very little, and scolded him for getting along so slowly. The fugitive received this, as he did everything, else, with stolid indifference.

Friend Brown did not know then, as everybody has learned since, that the slave, as a rule, did not do half as much work in the same time as a free man, and that habits of sloth thus formed, while in slavery, were not easily got rid of.

The storm continued through the day with unabated fury. Dark clouds came up from the eastward, seeming almost to touch the tops of the great oaks on Laurel hill, as they sailed through the heavy, cheerless atmosphere. The rain came down fitfully, sometimes in heavy gusts, and anon would subside for a few minutes into a gentle shower. The cattle came in early from the field and took shelter under the shedding behind the barn. The chickens wandered about in the rain, the tail feathers of the roosters draggling in the little pools that filled every hollow or inequality of the ground, and sought their roosts long before night came on. The little brook that coursed along the foot of Laurel hill was swollen into an angry flood, and the Octorara itself had risen so as to be hardly passable at the ford.

It was indeed a dull and gloomy day. Not a soul had been seen to pass along the road, though Mary's watchful eye was on the lookout the live-long day.

Before darkness settled down, however, the wind veered round to the north-west, and a streak of light in the direction of sunset indicated that the storm had subsided. The prospect was that the morrow would be clear.

It was no false promise. The morning was clear and cool, and with the first streak of light came Neddy. It was Seventh-day and he had come to "clean up" the wheat he had thrashed. This he could do by noon, and Neddy was opposed to working on Seventh-day afternoon, when he could avoid it.

He was informed that John was the fugitive of whom he had been told a few days before; and he looked at him with much the air that a well-to-do house dog would be supposed to regard a hungry cur who was quartered on him for the purpose of consuming a portion of his rations.

But his eye softened when it rested on Mary. He was a man of no mean penetration and he could not fail to observe her complete devotion to her child. Perhaps memory carried him back to a time when a dark-faced woman tended his little ones, and a soft, plaintive voice, now hushed forever, filled his humble home with pleasant music.

Neddy and John cleaned up the grain and put it into bags. They were done before noon, and Neddy walked down to the shop. "Well," said he "I'se done de wheat; guess I'll not work no more, to-day."

"How does the man do?" said Billy.

"He's no 'count, none uv 'em is. I'se tried 'em afore."

"Well," said Billy, "we must keep him a while, and he may as well do sumthin.' I want thee to thrash next week. On Second-day thee must thrash rye. Peggy Keys is a goin' to begin huskin' next week, and we must have rye straw for the fother Henry's goin' to Harford county on Second-day, with a new dearborn, and I want Sammy in the shop. John can help thee thrash the rye and when that is done him and the boys may go to the woods. They've got very little of the winter's wood cut yet."

Neddy was rather pleased that John was not to work with him much longer; but he still muttered something about him being "despit wuthless."

After dinner Neddy left, with the promise to return on Second-day morning. Before he started he informed his employer that he was in need of funds. He had worked five days and a half, and Billy went to his secretary, and unlocking it, took out five silver half dollars, and one quarter, and handed them to him. Neddy then left, and Billy promptly entered the payment, with a piece of chalk, on the partition close by the cellar-door.

In the afternoon Frank came running into the house; "Oh! mother," said he, "Grandfather Carter's a comin'."

"Is he?" said Margaret, "well, set the rocking-chair there in the corner for him."

The old man soon came in, and after the usual salutations, seated himself in his accustomed place. He visited Brown's frequently, and felt quite at home, seated near the broad fire-place, where he could squirt his tobacco juice without doing any particular damage. Margaret complained a little sometimes, after he had gone, about this filthy habit; but she had great regard for the old man and always treated him with the most profound respect.

Both these families were particularly careful in attending Friends' meeting. On First-day, especially, they insisted on all, who possibly could, to turn out. It was this that had brought him up to Brown's that afternoon.

"Margaret," said he, after being seated, as he placed both hands on the top of his silver-headed cane, and leaned his chin against them, "I see you've got some strangers."

"Yes," was the answer, "they came on Fifth-day night."

"They'll be with you some time, and it won't do very well for you all to go to meetin' to-morrow, and leave them here alone."

Margaret looked troubled. The idea of violence was unpleasant to her, and her mind reverted to the probability of a visit from slave-catchers. "Does thee think anybody'll come after 'em, grandfather?" she said.

"I've not heard of anybody being about, but we can't tell what might happen," said the old man, raising his head and squirting a great stream of tobacco juice diagonally across the fire, "we've got these people here and we ain't a goin' to have them carried back if we can help it."

"I don't know what father will say; Frank, call him and we'll see."

So Billy was called, and he agreed that the fugitives must not be left alone. It was settled that Henry and Sammy should stay at home, and the rest would go to meeting as usual.

But the quiet First-day passed away without an incident. No stranger appeared, and even Mary began to feel more secure. Grandfather Carter, on his long-legged horse "Bob," under pretense of talking to Billy about some wheel-wright stuff, rode round to Brown's ford to see that all was right, and looked quite satisfied when he saw the "boys" sitting quietly on the porch. Under ordinary circumstances they would have received a sound scolding for being absent from meeting.

Second day morning brought Neddy; and he and John went to work at the rye. Henry was up betimes and started for Harford county with the new dearborn. Ring had followed him, a circumstance which caused great grief to Frank when he awakened an hour or two afterward.

The day passed quietly away. Neddy quit work at sundown, and, closing the great barn-doors, started toward Carter's mill. "Till" had directed him to bring her some flour, and he knew better than to disobey. She had not proved herself a gentle and loving companion to him, but he always tried to keep the peace and get along as quietly as possible. So he was prompt to do whatever she required when it was within the bounds of reason.

After having his little bag filled with flour he placed it on his shoulder and started toward home. For some undefined reason he did not feel cheerful that evening. He had drawn out of John during the day some of the reasons why he had left his master, and his sympathies had been considerably excited. He had a great deal of contempt for him as a "pore wuthless critter," as he had for everybody who could not do a big day's work, but in spite of that he pitied him, and regretted that he had spoken harshly about him. But his warmest sympathies were excited for Mary. He observed her complete devotion to the child, and saw, to use his own words, that she was "a mighty clever kind of a woman." He also knew that the probabilities were that the slave-catchers, or "kidnappers," would be on their track, and already his mind was filled with schemes or plans for their protection, or release if captured.

Neddy walked swiftly forward on the road leading south from Carter's mill, until he crossed Black run and reached the foot of Goat hill; he then turned to the left, up a narrow path which led around the eastern side of the hill, through pines and black-jacks, in the direction of his humble home. Pursuing this for a hundred yards or more, he came to a narrow glen which indented the eastern side of the hill, and down which a little rivulet flowed; when, turning abruptly to the right, he followed the path toward the head of the glen, some fifty yards away.

Here was situated the rude log cabin which Neddy called his home. It was built of pine logs and covered with boards, and had but two apartments, a kitchen below and the attic above. The building was of the rudest kind, the kitchen floor being uneven and ricketty, and the walls simply pine logs, with the openings filled with clay. The apartment had but one window, composed of four small panes of glass, through which faint rays of light struggled into the dingy and desolate-looking room. The door was in keeping with the rest, being made of rude boards, poorly fitted together, and hung on wooden hinges. It was fastened on the inside with a wooden latch, and could be opened from the outside by a string, passed through a small hole for that purpose.

A few yards from the door of the hut, in a clump of tall pines, was a spring of clear, sweet water, from which the little rivulet to which we have referred flowed. Close by was a small lot fenced in for a garden, but beside this there was no evidence of cultivation within sight.

Neddy approached the hut, pulled the string on the outside, pushed open the door, which dragged heavily against the uneven floor, entered, and deposited his bag of flour on a rude bench near the door, saying:

"Here's yer flour."

This remark was addressed to his wife, Till, a woman some sixty years of age, to whom we have already referred.

She was quite dark, larger than ordinary women, and had a sullen and forbidding appearance. Dressed in clothes that had not lately seen the wash-tub, with a dark, dingy-looking cotton handkerchief bound around her head, she looked the very counterpart of the room in which she stood.

She made no reply, but looking sullenly into the fire of green pine, which burned slowly on the hearth, said:

"Ben's 'yer."

"Whar is 'e?" said Neddy with a start. "What's 'e doin yer?"

"Thar he is,' 'said Till, pointing to a dark corner of the room, where, on a low stool, sat a strapping, black, beastly-looking fellow, with an immense mouth, thick, flat head, and a vacant expression about the eyes indicating a low degree of mentality.

This was Ben Boodly, Till's son by a former marriage. He was a worthless creature, and led a wandering, vagabond life, sometimes not being seen in that neighborhood for months; then he would appear again and hang about Neddy's for weeks, much to the latter's disapprobation.

Ben would work a day or two now and then, but was generally idle, and it was a mystery to some who knew him how he managed to get along at all.

Neddy would gladly have forbidden him the house, but feared Till, who always took his part.

Neddy turned around and passed out at the door. He did not enjoy his home very much at the best; but when Ben was about, his discomfort was greatly increased.

A cool wind was blowing from the north-west, but the hill in the rear of the hut sheltered the little glen, and the air there was quite pleasant. There was no moon, but the stars shone out with unusual brilliancy, and not a cloud was to be seen. Neddy passed over to the clump of pines at the spring and sat down on a large stone, leaning his back against a stately pine.

His mind was disturbed and he felt unhappy.

The presence of Ben was always a source of irritation, and fears for the safety of the fugitives, that he knew to be in the neighborhood, occasioned him unrest. His mind reverted to the time when he had been a slave, and though well used, he shrank with horror from the idea of ever being in that condition again. He thought of Mary and her great devotion to the little one whom she had brought away from slavery; and his mind unconsciously reverted to the mother of his little ones who had long since passed away. Coming back to the present he thought of Till, her coarse, unfeeling behavior toward him, and the unhappy life he was forced to lead; and mentally contrasted the pleasure of his early wedded life with the present.

The wind sighed mournfully through the pines, and its low, gentle murmur, soothed his unquiet spirit. Far up on Goat hill the drowsy tinkling of a distant cow-bell sounded faintly on his ear. In the distance could be heard the dull roar of Carter's dam, as the water, still swollen by the recent rain, swept over its broad breast.

Neddy was tired, and these soothing sounds unconsciously lulled him to repose. The music of the pines sounded more and more faintly, the tinklings of the cow-bell were less and less perceptible, while the roar of the dam sunk into a whisper, and then ceased entirely--Neddy was asleep.

He slept long and soundly. When he awoke the stars told him that it was near midnight. He arose and entered the house. The fire smouldered on the hearth, and Till had gone to bed and was sound asleep. He lighted a lamp, which consisted of some lard in an old saucer, into which a piece of candle-wick had been placed, to look for Ben. He examined the kitchen and ascended into the loft, out could not find him.

Ben had gone.

With a muttered imprecation on that "wuthless critter," Neddy retired to his bed.

The Brown family were, as usual, seated in front of the broad kitchen fire-place that evening. As the last faint ray of daylight disappeared in the west, a knock was heard at the kitchen door, and in response to the invitation to "come in," the door opened, and Joe Simmons entered. He had in one hand a double-barrelled shot-gun, and around his shoulders were slung powder-horn and shot-pouch. In the other hand he carried a couple of fine-looking gray squirrels which had fallen victims to his unerring aim.

"Why, Joe," said Margaret, running to the door and holding out her hand, "how is thee; I'm so glad to see thee."

Billy was less demonstrative, but Joe was a great favorite of his. He extended a cordial welcome, and taking his gun and powder and shot, laid them away, while Joe took a seat near the fire.

"Well, Peggy," said Joe, after being seated, "how is she? Here, I've brought her a couple of squirrels to make a pot-pie. I come down on purpose to eat one of her pot-pies.

"Yes, I'll make thee a pot-pie; but thee ain't had supper?"

"No, I haven't, that's a fact," said Joe, laughing, "can she get me some?"

"Yes, indeed, we'll have it ready in a little while."

So while they are getting supper, we will make our readers better acquainted with Joe Simmons.

They already know that he is a bachelor, and that Margaret was his housekeeper before her marriage with William Brown. No better hearted, cleverer fellow ever lived than Joe; but in many respects he was a most eccentric creature. He had been raised a Friend, but had become a confirmed Free-thinker, and did not attempt the slightest concealment of that fact. Indeed, he openly spoke of having read the works of Paine, Voltaire and Volney, and defended their doctrines. He would talk and argue all day on the subject of theology, if opportunity offered, neglecting important business matters for that purpose. He was quite well read on general subjects, and no mean opponent in a discussion. He often attended neighboring debating clubs, and was noted for his profusion of quaint, curious illustrations, which usually produced great merriment among the listeners. He was remarkably gentle and kind-hearted, and Margaret Brown, who had known him long and well, was accustomed to say that "no honester man ever broke bread."

He had a habit of talking a great deal about getting himself a wife, and was constantly promising to pay his addresses to one and another; but it was pretty well ascertained that Joe had never made the slightest attempt at courting in his life.

He was a great sportsman. Hunting was his delight, and there was no surer shot, or one who understood the habits of game better, in that section of country, than Joe Simmons.

While supper was being prepared, Billy and Joe talked over old times; at length, looking at the two fugitives, Joe said:

"Who's these people thee's got here, Billy?"

"Some that Davy brought along," was the reply.

Looking closely at Mary, he observed her anxious and eager face, and said: "She need'nt be afraid to-night. I've got a couple of good loads in that gun there; either of 'em would fetch a kidnapper. I'll keep 'em off to-night."

"Come now," said Margaret, "supper's ready."

After supper Mary and John went to bed. Margaret and Martha put away the things, and then the latter also left, taking Frank, who had, as usual, fallen asleep. The apprentice went to his room, and Joe was left with Margaret and Billy.

The three fell into conversation. "Where's Henry?" inquired Joe.

"Gone to Harford with a new dearborn. He took the dog along, too. Ring ought to be here tonight."

"Oh, I reckon there's no danger to-night," said Joe. "But Billy, does thee know that it is out about runaways bein' here? That's what brought me down."

"Who knows it?" said both in one breath.

Joe looked more serious than he had yet done, and said in low tones, "Sam Doan."

"Merciful Creator!" exclaimed Margaret, "does that wretch know it? Is thee sure he does?"

58

"Yes, I'm sure. The hired man who works for me drinks a little sometimes, and last night he was on a spree over at Twaddle's. Sam was there, pretty well corned, and the man heard him telling a stranger, who was a pretty hard-lookin' fellow too, that there was some runaway niggers at Billy Brown's. He told me this morning.

Margaret looked deeply distressed. She knew Sam Doan, and knew him to be a reckless outlaw, who feared neither God nor man. He had been the terror of her childhood and youth, and her cheek blanched with fear whenever she chanced to meet him in the public highway. She had not a doubt that he would assist to kidnap these poor creatures, if by so doing he could secure a reward.

"It's in bad hands," said Billy, "that's sartin. I must see Davy to-morrow, and tell him about it.

"Yes," remarked Joe, "Davy understands these matters better than any of us. I never knew him to fail in a case yet. He'd better be seen pretty soon."

The conversation then changed. "Peggy," said Joe, "does thee go to meetin' as reg'lar as ever?"

"Yes, I go whenever I can."

"She used to go very reg'lar when she kep' house for me," said he, laughing, "but I thought mebby she wouldn't care so much about it after she got married."

This was almost too much for a joke, but Margaret laughed it off. Joe was always permitted to say what he chose.

"I've been readin' a good deal of Elias Hicks' works this fall," pursued Joe, "they're mighty interestin'."

"How does thee like 'em?" said Margaret, hoping that his views of religion had undergone a change.

"Well, I like 'em purty well. Elias has some very good idees. He's a great improvement on the ancient Friends, but I don't think his doctrines are quite as sound as Paine's."

Margaret looked deeply shocked. She had a warm, sisterly affection for the good-hearted fellow; but his notions of religion gave her intense pain.

"Oh! Joe, how can thee talk so. Thee wasn't brought up with such dreadful notions. What would thy mother say if she was here, to hear such talk? I'm sure Elias Hicks believed every word of the Scriptures."

"If he did he'd a poor way of tellin' it. But he was a great man, I admit that."

"He believed it in his way," interrupted Billy, "he spiritualized some passages."

"Yes," said Joe, "if a man was allowed to explain everything to suit himself he could believe all that was ever written."

Margaret was anxious to change the subject, so she remarked that it was ten o'clock, and proposed that they should go to bed. To this all agreed, Joe remarking that "her and Billy used to sit up a good deal later at his house, when Billy came there to buy wheelwright stuff."

Joe carried his gun up-stairs and told them to give him a call if he was needed. Billy and Margaret retired and lay awake some time talking over the unpleasant news they had received.

CHAPTER VII.
A FOOT-RACE.

"Night's silent reign had robbed the world of light;
To lend, in lieu, a greater benefit,
Repose and sleep: when every mortal breast
Whom care or grief permitted, took their rest."

BILLY BROWN could not divest himself of the feeling that something unpleasant would happen before long. This was rather an impression, for which he could give no adequate cause, than a conviction founded on reason. He knew Sam Doan and regarded him as a reckless, unprincipled creature; but he had never heard of his being engaged in or connected with the business of kidnapping. He knew Margaret's utter abhorrence of the man; but attributed this in a great measure to prejudice formed in childhood, and thought it, perhaps, unjust in her to jump at once to the conclusion that he would assist in giving information or in capturing the fugitives. Still he thought the case, as he had said, was in bad hands, and he resolved to lose no time in letting Davy know about it. With this resolve in his mind he fell asleep.

He awakened with the conviction that something had disturbed his rest. He listened, and a scarcely perceptible sound, as of some one moving about in the kitchen below, attracted his attention. He raised his head, and reaching over the side of the bed, bent his ear in the direction from whence it came. It still continued at intervals, and the conviction gained strength in his mind that some person was there. It could not be the cat, she would not be moving about unless in search of rats, and then she would be more noiseless in her movements; it must be some person. He resolved to see.

Slipping quietly out of bed, he softly opened the door of his room and glided down-stairs. There was but a thin board partition between him and the kitchen, and he heard movements more distinctly, and was convinced that some one was there. He was barefoot, and had nothing on but his night-shirt, but for this there was no remedy. Any attempt to return and dress himself, or even to put on his shoes, would alarm the intruder and result in his escape. He determined to run no risk of this kind; his object being to bag the game if possible. Gliding silently to the bottom of the stairway, he reached out his hand to unlatch the door. A little excitement, probably, unsteadied his hand, or, peradventure, he was rather hasty in his anxiety to get a glimpse at the uninvited occupant of the kitchen; at any rate he did not succeed in opening the door noiselessly; the latch clicked, and there was a quick movement and a rush across the floor. He pushed the door open just in time to see the form of a man getting out at the front window. Billy made for the door, but he had to draw the long wooden bolt with which it was fastened and this gave the fellow a start. There was no moon, but the night was clear and there was sufficient starlight to distinguish objects at a short distance. He fancied, as he caught a glimpse of the man clambering through the window, that he carried a bundle of things in his arms and inferred that he had stolen them. When the door was opened the thief was outside of the yard, and had started up the road in the direction of Carter's mill. Friend Brown went for him. He was now fully aroused, and the cause was one that demanded his best efforts. On they went, pursuer and pursued, each one straining every nerve and doing his level best.

The wood which intervened between Brown's and Carter's mill was a half mile or more long, and traversed by a narrow road, rough and stony. Two-thirds of this distance was level, and then a hill succeeded, at the top of which the wood terminated. Into this wood they plunged, the Quaker in his night-shirt, his black locks streaming in the wind, and the cold, rough ground and sharp stones, with which the road abounded, telling fearfully on his bare feet. The thief, who was a powerful man and swift of foot, strained every muscle to distance his pursuer. But the load of plunder which he carried began to tell against him. Ere they had gone a hundred yards his pursuer had recovered half the distance lost at the start, and was gaining rapidly. Dismayed at this, he began to drop, one by one, the articles he had taken, but he had carried them too long; the extra weight affected his wind, and the Quaker still slowly gained. By this time the pursuer's feet were growing sore, and his pluck had lost its first keen edge; but still he cherished not the slightest intent of giving up the chase. When they reached the foot of the hill the thief looked back over his shoulder, and saw the Quaker's night-shirt, like a wandering spirit, fluttering in the darkness close behind him. His renewed fears overcame his greed, and he dropped his entire load and sped forward with all his energies.

Friend Brown, too, confident that the prey was now within his grasp, called up every latent energy, and, regardless of his bleeding, lacerated feet, and the stones that bruised and cut them at every step, urged himself forward, inspired by the hope of a speedy triumph. Up the hill these two toiled, the pursuer slowly gaining. Just as they reached the top he felt secure of triumph. He was close behind the thief, and felt that he had him secure. Reaching out his hand and placing it on the fellow's shoulder, he yelled (disregarding the language of Friends entirely), "Stop, you scoundrel!" This was his great mistake, as it was the other's safety. Instead of obeying, he made a flank movement by jumping to one side, and then, darting forward with renewed speed, left the Quaker far behind.

Friend Brown felt that the race was over, and that he must retrace his steps. This was no easy job; his feet were bruised and bleeding, and numb with cold. The excitement was over, and at every step he felt intense pain. Every time he ventured forward he could scarcely repress an exclamation of pain. He went into the woods, and sitting down on some moss by the root of a great tree, took off his shirt and wrapped up his feet in it. He pressed it against them and warmed and soothed them as well as he could, and then started on his homeward journey. He kept in the woods, away from the road, where the ground was soft and where the fallen leaves afforded some protection to his feet, and slowly made his way to the house. When he reached there he found the door open and the window up just as they had been left. Not a soul had been awakened but himself; so he quietly closed the door, let down the window, and after warming himself by the coals on the hearth went back to bed as quietly as he had left it.

In the morning he called to the apprentice, who had the fire made before daylight, and telling what had happened, directed him when it was light to go over the road and pick up such articles as he could find scattered along it.

He returned just as the family were sitting down to breakfast, with an armful of various kinds of things. There were pairs of stockings, balls of woolen-yarn, skeins of flax-yarn, pairs of mittens, combs, large pieces of bread and meat, and many other articles that the thief had taken but dropped in his flight. Margaret declared, after a careful examination, that every article taken had been recovered. He had not kept a single thing; indeed, he had lost his hat, a white wool one, which the apprentice also found and brought back with him.

Joe Simmons laughed immoderately when he heard of the night's adventure. He was as much pleased with the fact that the intruder was not after the fugitives, as he was amused at the odd and exciting race that had taken place.

When Neddy came he was told of the affair, and shown the lost hat. "Does thee know whose it is?" asked Billy.

Neddy looked at it carefully for some time and then said: "Ye--yes, I do, ging-god, it's Ben's."

"What Ben?"

"Be--Ben Boodley's."

Neddy then told of Ben being at his house the night before, and leaving early in the night. All hands agreed that Ben was the thief. Indeed, Billy, who knew him, remembered now that the man he had pursued very much resembled Ben in general appearance.

All hands, however, agreed that inasmuch as the stolen articles had all been recovered, and Ben badly frightened, that it was just as well to let the affair drop. He would leave the neighborhood and not likely return for several months; at any rate he would not venture into Billy Brown's kitchen very soon again.

Neddy and John went to work again at thrashing the rye. Billy said he could not go to see Davy till Henry returned, which would be about noon; his feet were too sore to walk and his only horse was away.

Henry came back a little before noon. He had met with good luck; everything had gone well; and the man was well pleased with his job. He incidentally mentioned, in speaking of his journey, that he had met Sam Doan in the neighborhood of Conowingo bridge, going in that direction.

Margaret's cheek paled. Joe Simmons and Billy looked at each other meaningly but said nothing.

After a pause the latter remarked: "Henry, feed the horse an' rub him down carefully. I think I'll use him this afternoon."

Margaret had killed a chicken, and with it and the squirrels Joe Simmons had brought, made a superb pot-pie for dinner. Joe praised it highly, at which she evinced a great deal of quiet satisfaction.

After dinner Joe left, much to the regret of the whole family. He declared, however, he would be down again "to-morrow night." At present he could stay no longer.

Billy went to the stable after dinner and brought out the horse. He looked so tired and weary he could not think of riding him. He wanted to see Davy, and his feet were too sore to walk. What would he do? He resolved to send Neddy.

Calling him out of the barn, he entrusted him with the whole story, and told of the suspicions he had with regard to an attempt being made for the re-capture of the fugitives. He closed by directing him to tell Davy all about it, and to say nothing to any one else unless directed by him to do so. He was to come back that night and report.

John and the boys were sent out to continue the cutting of the winter's fire-wood; the barn-doors were closed, the flails hung in their places, and Friend Brown went to work, as usual, in the shop.

Mary had listened to the account of the night's adventure with a good deal of attention and no small degree of alarm. True, it was evident that the man was only a thief, and probably knew nothing of fugitive slaves being in the neighborhood. But the fact remained that there was some one lurking about the premises at night, and this was to her cause for alarm. Every incident of an unusual character produced anxiety in her mind. If the dog barked she feared some one was coming to carry away her child. If a stranger approached she saw in him a kidnapper to bear him back to slavery. The fact that the house had been visited and entered at night served to deepen her anxiety and increase her unhappiness.

Some time during the afternoon Mary was assisting Margaret in hanging out some clothes they had washed; little Charlie was sitting on the kitchen floor, looking at some block houses that Frank was building for his amusement; Mary's watchful eye discovered in the distance some half dozen persons approaching by the road which passed in front of the barn. Quick as thought she leaped from the chair on which she was standing, bounded into the kitchen, and snatching up Charlie, clasped him convulsively to her breast, and rushed into the stairway leading into the cellar. Here she seated herself upon the topmost step, presenting such a picture of absolute, perfect terror as no human language can describe.

It was an embodiment of dumb, speechless agony that defies the proper use of words to convey any adequate conception of. It was not ordinary fear or fright--it was not a concern for personal safety--it was the surging waves of a woman's soul, stirred to their profoundest depths by a mother's love, and a mother's fear for the safety of her child.

It is remarkable how deeply some incidents are impressed upon the mind in childhood. It is then more susceptible, and the impressions are more enduring than in after life. Affairs that are readily forgotten by persons grown to man's estate, imbed themselves in the recollection of children and are fresh and green in them through life, often exercising most important influence in the formation of their characters.

Frank, who was seated on the floor, looked at the woman in blank amazement. He saw that she was alarmed and he felt that she was under the influence of some powerful feeling, but he understood nothing more. He never, however, forgot her expression of speechless agony, and in after years, when he had grown to manhood, could call it up in all its freshness, and to his mind's eye the picture was as perfect as when he first saw it. Then he could analyze it. Then he could understand that the Demon of Slavery, crushing beneath its pitiless tread millions of human souls, was simply burying that mother's heart under its remorseless footsteps.

Many a time in after life, when in the storm of pro-slavery darkness and vengeance that swept over the land, social and political standing and even personal safety were imperiled by opposition to slavery, and he was sometimes tempted to yield to what seemed to be the decrees of fate, the recollection of that slave mother's mutely pleading, unspoken agony, nerved his heart to renewed and continued effort against the hell-born institution.

Margaret passed into the room and said to Mary, as gently as she could, that she "guessed" there was no danger; but the woman looked up to her imploringly, and she retired.

Going to the end of the porch next to the shop, she said quietly to her husband that he had better come to the house for a few minutes. He did so, and remained until the strangers went by. They had no intention of disturbing any one; but had been at a camp-meeting some two or three miles south and chose that road to return.

Mary came out after she was assured they had passed, but seemed unusually nervous and excited the rest of the day.

During the afternoon Peggy Keys and Tommy passed by the shop, she sitting in an ox-cart and Tommy driving. They had been over the creek of an errand and were on their way home. They stopped, and Peggy went into the shop to light her pipe. After puffing at it a minute or two, she said: "Well, Billy, thee wouldn't trust me enough to tell me what Old Josey was here for that day, but I found it out. I know it wasn't any of my bus'ness, but thee needn't been afeard of me. I was down at the mill a few days after and was settin' in the mill-room at the fire, waitin' for a grist, and I he'rd Brister Wilson, the miller, and grandfather talking about it outside. They talked it all over, but I never let on. I never told a breath of it, not even to Tommy. I never tell things, Billy," she continued, raising her voice and looking at him rather reproachfully, "that I know ought to be kep'. There's never a livin' creetur will get a whimper of that out of me. I hope the poor things 'ill get off safe."

Billy felt badly. He knew full well that she had a good heart, and had only feared that she would unintentionally let the matter out. He now regretted he had not made a confidant of her, and impressed her with the importance of silence.

Tommy, who had grown tired of waiting, now came to the door and asked if she "was 'most ready to go?"

"Not quite. I'll be there in a minnet or two. Mind the oxen, Tommy. Thee'd better hold on to the rope; they might run away.

Tommy went back, seized the rope, which was tied around the head of the near ox, and awaited her coming.

"Where's Sam Doan live now?" inquired Billy.

"He lives in the barrens, about three miles away from us; but he's not often at home. He follows coalin'. I guess he's over in Lancaster county somewhere," was the reply.

"They say he knows about these people bein' here."

"I shouldn't wonder. He finds out things from some of the wust of the blacks. He runs with 'em and 'sociates with 'em, and gits 'em to drinkin' and then he'll pick out of 'em ennything he wants. He's a bad man, Billy, and he's cunnin' as a fox."

Billy fell into a study, and Peggy re-lighted her pipe and started out, bidding him farewell, with the remark that they would "begin the corn in a day or two."

When the boys and John returned in the evening, Henry related that on their way out they had seen a man approaching them some distance off, on the road they were going. As soon as John discovered him, without saying a word, he dropped his ax, and leaping the fence at one bound struck off into the forest with the speed of a deer. Here, secreting himself, he remained until the stranger had passed out of sight, when he came slowly back. There was not the slightest occasion for alarm, as the man was a neighbor who lived a mile or two away; but so thoroughly were these fugitives terrified, that every sight and sound occasioned renewed alarm.

Neddy came back after dark, and calling Billy out, told him that Davy had been fully informed of all the particulars. Indeed, he knew them pretty well before, having heard of Sam Doan going over into Maryland, which was of itself suspicious. He had very little doubt that the slave-hunters would be over soon, perhaps to-morrow; but he thought there was no danger of them coming to-night. It would be well, however, to keep a lookout. He had men on the watch who would let him know if any suspicious persons crossed Conowingo bridge. He thought when they did come they would cross during the day and put up somewhere near the line, starting from there after night and expecting to get back with the fugitives before morning. This was his judgment of their movements, founded on considerable experience, and a knowledge of the locality of the owners of John and Mary.

In the meantime he proposed a place of concealment for them, to which they should be removed, when it was ascertained that their owners were in search of them. Until that time it was best they should remain where they were.

Neddy was told by Davy to give all the information he had obtained to Grandfather Carter and Bristow Wilson, whose co-operation in what was to follow must be secured. This he had already done, and the only thing to do now was to wait until news came from Davy. The moment he believed the slave-hunters were within reach he would send word, with all the particulars and directions how to act.

This was his statement, made in bad English, with a good deal of stammering, and frequent interpolations of "ging-god" and other words of that character; but it possessed clearness and force and was, withal, as the listener well knew, perfectly reliable.

Neddy was then invited in to supper, which he ate in silence and started for his home.

As the name of Bristow Wilson has been mentioned once or twice in this chapter, and as he plays an important part in the incidents that are about to occur, we will introduce him more fully to our readers.

Bristow Wilson, or as he was called in the neighborhood, "Brister," was the miller at Carter's mill. He was to all appearance a full-blooded African, black as the shades of night, with thick lips, broad, flat nose, and short, kinky hair. He was a large, powerful man, broad-shouldered and squarely built, and looked the very impersonation of vigorous health and physical enjoyment. His head was large, his forehead broad and high, the coronal region well-developed, while his clear, honest eye at once attracted attention and secured confidence. He had been raised by Grandfather Carter from a child, and treated by him with the utmost kindness and consideration. Indeed, everybody treated "Brister," as he was called, well. It seemed impossible to do otherwise. At that time, when a bitter prejudice against color was almost universal, he was treated by every resident in the neighborhood, man and woman, as though he were a full-blooded Caucasian. Nobody ever seemed to think of his color. It has often been a puzzle to the writer of this how it was, but such is the undeniable fact. He was extremely social and kindhearted; but he never transgressed the strict bounds of propriety. He was scrupulously honest, and his integrity was never known to have been called in question. The most aristocratic people in that section treated him with careful consideration. Indeed, he seemed to have that quiet, unaffected dignity that always compels respect. Bristow possessed such an education as was common with the well-to-do-people of that locality, and was quite intelligent. As a matter of course he sympathized with those of his race who were in slavery, and being a man of discretion and courage, was a very proper confidant of those who were planning for the safety of the fugitives in the impending struggle.

CHAPTER VIII.
THE DESERTED HOUSE.

"Life and thought have gone away
Side by side,
Leaving door and windows wide;
Careless tenants they!"

THE Octoraro, in its passage from Brown's ford to Carter's, described the arc of a circle, while the public road connecting the two places was nearly in a straight line. By the stream the distance between the two points was more than a mile; but by the highway it was much less.

Along the southern bank of the creek was a continuous forest, which we have already described, reaching four-fifths of the distance. The most of this, for a considerable distance from the stream, was covered with an undergrowth, mainly of laurel, so thick as to be almost impenetrable except where traversed by footpaths, of which there were a few, known only to those who frequented the banks of the stream for hunting and fishing purposes.

On the northern bank, for a considerable distance below the ford at Brown's, the land was cleared and under cultivation. Then followed a forest-covered hill, which rose abruptly from the stream, and along whose steep and rugged side the traveler could only clamber by following a narrow and tortuous path, clinging the while to such bushes and trees as came within his reach. After this came a space of cleared land, entirely inclosed by a forest, and then succeeded another wood, the counterpart of that we have been describing.

The cleared spot of land, to which we have referred, ran back a short distance from the creek, and was bounded in that direction by the wood.

It was thus inclosed by woodland on three sides, while in its front ran the Octorara, so deep as not to be fordable at this point, in consequence of the water being backed up by the dam, not more than half a mile below.

The spot embraced some four or five acres, and was much less hilly than the land either above or below it. Across it, from north to south, dividing it in two almost equal parts, ran a little valley or "hollow," through which flowed a small rivulet of pure water, which reached the level of the creek a few yards from its banks by means of a "tumble" or small waterfall, where its clear, bright waters were poured into an inlet or cove several feet deep. This was a favorite fishing ground for those who frequented the banks of the stream for that purpose.

Along the creek, in front of the clearing to which we have referred, was a wilderness of bushes and briars several feet deep; these reached close to the edge of the little inlet we have been describing, on either side, shutting it out of view from almost every point on both sides of the stream.

On the western slope of this clearing, near the edge of the wood, and fronting the Octorara, stood an old, deserted house. It was a small log building, and had a neglected, dilapidated appearance. Years before it had been inhabited by a family of negroes, but of late had been entirely unoccupied.

The place had that forlorn and woe-begone look that ever belongs to a deserted habitation. The spot that had once been used as a garden was overgrown with weeds, which choked and smothered down the few bright flowers that struggled upward for a brief existence. Rank weeds grew up at the sides of the house, whose tops met the ends of the long slabs of which the roof was made, forming a harbor for snakes and other reptiles. Around the old stone chimney, and on the ends of the logs which stood out at the corners, were dilapidated birds' nests, that having served their purpose were abandoned. The door, which was in the gable-end opposite the chimney, stood ajar, having been left so by some wandering fishermen or hunters whom curiosity had prompted to open it and look inside. The wind had partly loosened some of the slabs of which the roof was made, and they hung, listlessly, awaiting another gale to hurl them to the ground.

Inside, the floor was reasonably good, while the broad fire-place looked as though waiting hungrily for the long-delayed supply of wood; three or four rude benches, probably left there by the former occupants, made up the furniture of the room.

It was as lonely a spot as could well be imagined. No road, public or private, came within reach of it. It was surrounded on three sides by deep forests, and was only approachable by narrow, rugged and almost inaccessible paths. In front flowed the Octorara, not fordable at that place, nor for a long distance, up or down. On the opposite bank was the deep, dark wood already described; and there the creek could only be approached on foot and by those who were familiar with the narrow and intricate paths. Not a human dwelling was in sight, not a cultivated field, not a single mark of civilization. It was lonely, and wild, and desolate; indeed, only those quite familiar with the neighborhood knew of its existence at all.

It was this place that Davy McCann, whose mind was always on the alert, and who was intimately acquainted with every foot of ground in that section of country, had decided upon as a temporary hiding-place for the fugitives, as soon as it became certain that the slave-hunters were in pursuit of them.

He rightly conjectured that when they received information of the whereabouts of the runaways, they would not attempt to retake them in day-time, but would approach the place at night, both because it would be easier then to capture them, and there would be less danger of a rescue while they were being conveyed away.

Neither did he think it good policy to have them started farther north at present. Pursuit would inevitably be made, which might be successful. It was much better that they should be secreted near by, and the pursuers, who would naturally suppose they had left the neighborhood, thus thrown off their guard.

He therefore directed Neddy to convey them to this spot when intelligence should be forwarded to him that it was necessary for them to move; but that under no circumstances should they be removed in day-time; the trip should be made at night. This, he said, could be readily done, as there was not the slightest danger that the slave-catchers would make their appearance at Brown's until some time after nightfall. These directions Neddy had conveyed to Billy Brown as well as Grandfather Carter and Bristow Wilson.

So well convinced was Neddy that the next night would bring with it important events, that he determined to begin preparations at once. On his way home he stopped to see Bristow Wilson, at the mill, and the two went into the little room together and sat down on the low bench by the fire, where the subject was carefully talked over.

A boat or scow was kept on the dam for carrying stones and earth to repair the breast; it was also used for fishing purposes. This, it was agreed, should be moved up the stream to a point opposite the deserted house, on the evening of the next day, to be in readiness for conveying the fugitives across. Neddy, in the meantime, who was familiar with the way, would conduct them, as soon as it was dark, through the wood on the southern bank to where the boat was in readiness and have them ferried over.

So far all seemed fair sailing. It was deemed important, however, that some preparation should be made at the house for their reception. The nights were not by any means warm, and with only the bare floor and two or three benches it was a bad place for a woman and child to remain all night; and it was quite possible they would be compelled to stay there even longer.

After some consultation it was resolved that the place should be visited that night, and the necessary preparations made. This could be done more readily by going up in the boat than by any other method; and that the two men resolved to do.

Bristow, having finished the grist he was grinding, shut down the gate and proceeded to close up the mill, first providing himself with a few matches and a tallow candle to be used when they reached their destination.

Just as they stepped outside and were closing the door, a horse came round the corner of the building with a bag across his back and a well-grown negro perched on top of it.

"Hilloa!" said Bristow, "ha! ha! a purty time o' night to be coming to mill; what ye got there, Jem?"

"Got sum weat; the'r putty near out o' flour an' I've got to go 'way with the team to-morrer; had to cum."

"All right, give me a lift and we'll put her in."

This man was Jem Body, an active young colored man, who lived with a farmer about a mile north of the deserted house. He was a good hand and quite trusty, but very fond of dancing, and attended all the parties at the houses of colored people for miles around.

"Neddy," said Bristow, who did not relish the idea of going on the proposed journey if it could be avoided, "here's the very man we want. Jem can go over to the old house and fix things to-night; it's not far for him when he gets home."

"What d' ye want at the ole house; be dern'd if I can go to-night," said Jem.

The matter was then explained to Jem; and the necessity of having something arranged to make it more comfortable for the woman and child was urged.

"I can't go, I tell ye I can't. There's a party I promist to go to, an' I must go; won't it do to-morrer nite?"

"No," said Bristow, "it had better be done now. We'd better have all these things done now, so we can be on the lookout then."

"Sorry I can't 'comodate ye, but I promist to go, and I mus go."

Here they plainly saw there was no use in any further persuasion, and admonishing Jem that he must keep his mouth shut on the subject, he was allowed to depart.

When he had gone Neddy seemed much excited: "Gi--ging-god," said he, "I--I wish we hadn't sed nothin' to 'im."

"Never mind," said Bristow, "he'll not say a word. "He's a purty quiet, safe kind of a darkey."

"Ye--yes, I know he is; but ging-god, he's a goin' after that gal at Porter's, an' he'll mebby tell her, an' she'll think it's too big a thing to keep, an' she'll tell somebody else."

"O, I guess not; now we'd better be off."

So the two started; going first to the barn, they rolled together two bundles of straw and tied them up with some pieces of rope, and then carried them across to the dam where the boat was fastened to a tree by a small chain. They placed the bundles of straw in the boat, unfastened it, and by the aid of a pole commenced moving up stream. The distance was not much over half a mile, and they were not long in reaching the place. Here they moored the boat in the little cove already spoken of, and throwing the straw out on the bank, jumped out themselves, and fastening the chain to a small maple that grew near, clambered up the bank, and with the straw on their shoulders proceeded toward the deserted house.

Entering it, they laid their loads on the floor and proceeded to strike a light. Everything looked gloomy and desolate, but they had no time to contemplate it. Neddy took out his pocket-knife, and running the small blade through the candle, stuck it into the side of one of the benches, so that it answered in place of a candlestick. They then went out to the edge of the forest and gathered up a quantity of dead wood, breaking it in convenient lengths, and carried it into the house. After they had gathered what they thought was sufficient, they brought in two good-sized stones and laid them on the hearth to serve in lieu of andirons. They then placed the bundles of straw, which were intended to serve for a bed for the fugitives, in one corner of the room, and carefully putting out the candle, closed the door and started for the boat.

Their passage back was without incident, but when they were on shore again Bristow said:

"Neddy, it's late, and the night's cool, would a drop of the critter hurt us?"

"N--no 't would'nt," said Neddy, "ef we had it," he added, doubtfully.

"I have a little at the house, let's go and try it."

So the two proceeded to the little log house in which Bristow lived, and a bottle was produced, out of which the two drank. Bristow tasted it carefully, but Neddy took a long and delicious swallow, apparently prolonging the effort for the purpose of affording himself additional gratification:

"That's de thing, ging-god, it goes jest to de place."

Bristow looked at his watch and said it was after eleven o'clock. Neddy started home and he retired to bed.

Early the next morning Davy McCann arrived with information that the owners of John and Mary had crossed Conowingo bridge the night before, and put up the tavern near the Maryland line. He was fully informed of their movements and intentions by a spy who had been lounging about there for several days, and whom no one suspected. The owners were in a light two-horse wagon and were accompanied by two men on horseback, making four in all. They would remain there until dark in order to excite no suspicion, and then start for Brown's, where they had been informed the fugitives were. After taking possession of them they would return to Maryland that night.

Davy was informed, by Bristow, of the arrangements that had been made, and fully approved them. He advised that the fugitives should leave Brown's as soon as it was dark that evening, but not before; and that a sharp lookout should be kept on the slave-hunters, both as they approached and as they left the neighborhood.

Neddy came along on his way to Brown's, and was told what news Davy had brought. He was not surprised, indeed he had anticipated it, and was much gratified that preparations had been made that would, in all probability, prevent John and Mary from being captured.

It was a day of great uneasiness at Brown's. A sense of impending evil seemed to oppress all the members of the family. Those who understood the matter felt convinced that the slave-hunters would be foiled, but would not divest themselves of a vague, undefined uneasiness for which no adequate reason could be given. The fugitives were told that they would have to move that night, and that their owners were upon their track. John received the information with the same stolid look he had always shown; but Mary exhibited a deeper earnestness in her countenance, and kept her eye more intensely fixed upon Charley, who seemed to be the very center of her being.

Though the night had been cool the day was bright and pleasant. Early in the forenoon Frank came running into the house, singing: "Grand--father Car--ter's a com--min', with a bun--dle un--der his a--r--m," and sure enough he appeared in a few minutes, trudging along with a large roll under his arm.

Entering the kitchen and taking his accustomed seat, he asked for Mary.

"She's up-stairs," said Margaret.

"Call her down," was the reply, "I want to see her."

So Mary was called, and in a few minutes, with Charley in her arms, made her appearance.

"Here's something for thee, when thee goes out to-night," said the kind-hearted, but somewhat stern old man, as he unrolled the package and exhibited a thick, warm and most substantial shawl, such as was then worn by Friends, "try it on and she how it suits thee."

Mary hesitated, but Margaret picked it up and unfolded it. As she did so a small package wrapped up in paper fell out. She then threw it around Mary's shoulders.

"What a nice shawl. I think I've seen it before, Grandfather."

"Yes, thee has. It belonged to one who'll never wear it again. But dead people," continued the old man, though his voice trembled a little, "don't wear shawls. It is the livin' we must take care of." Mary was silent. Presently grandfather picked up the package that had fallen, and unwrapping it took out a pair of strong, well-made little shoes. Holding them out he said: "These are for the little boy; put them on him, I want to see how they fit."

Charley was seated on a chair, and the pair of old socks he had been wearing were taken off and the shoes put on in their places. They were quite large, but this grandfather pronounced a "good fault."

The boy was intensely gratified, which he manifested by a continued broad grin. His mother felt very grateful, and wanted to express her thanks, but had not the power to utter them. While she was lacing them up, two large, bright tears rolled down her cheeks and fell on the little feet; the only manifestation of gratitude she had the power to make.

Grandfather Carter noticed this and turned away his face; placing both hands on the top of his cane and resting his chin against them, he gazed long and earnestly into the kitchen fire. He was experiencing that purest of all joys, the consciousness of having done a good act that was gratefully appreciated. The gratitude of that poor slave-mother was more precious to him than all the wealth or fame that a monarch could have laid at his feet. It was a bliss that no earthly power could deprive him of. Soon rising, he bade farewell and returned home.

In the evening supper was had before the usual time, but Mary could not eat; John, however, ate as usual, while Neddy manifested considerable uneasiness. He felt that the time for action had arrived. When supper was over, Mary had the shawl thrown around her, while Charley was wrapped in a little cloak that had once been Frank's. This, with his new shoes, made him look quite comfortable.

It was arranged that Henry should go to the dam and bring the boat up to the point opposite the deserted house, while Neddy and the apprentice should accompany the fugitives through the woods and meet him at that place.

Henry accordingly started off as soon as supper was over, while the rest waited for night's curtain to throw its protecting shield around them before venturing out. As soon, however, as it was quite dark they started, with kind farewells and many a silent prayer that no harm should overtake them.

The night was bright and beautiful. The stars looked down to earth as kindly as though no accursed system of wrong crushed millions beneath its iron heel. The new moon showed a narrow crescent of light, that just skirted the western hill and struggled through the foliage of the deep forest.

They pursued the road over which Billy Brown had chased the frightened burglar a few nights before, until they reached the top of the hill where he had given up the chase. Then, turning to the right, they passed along the edge of a wood for a short distance, and plunged into the forest. Neddy, who knew the path well, took the lead, followed by Mary, who all the time carried her boy, not permitting any one to take him from her. John walked next to her, and the apprentice brought up the rear.

Down through the dark and almost pathless forest, over rocks and stones, through bushes seemingly impenetrable, they went, until at last they emerged from the thick undergrowth and could see the bright waters of the Octorara gleaming through the interstices of the forest.

Neddy was a superb guide. He struck the exact spot intended, and found Henry with the boat awaiting them.

"Now, boys," said he, "dey'll mebby want you at de house. We's all safe enuff. You better git back as soon as ye kin."

Henry and the apprentice started at once, and knowing the way very well, were soon far on their way home.

Neddy took hold of the chain and drew the boat alongside of a fallen tree at the water's edge; he then gave John the end, and getting in, told Mary to hand the boy to him. She reluctantly consented. He then with one hand assisted her into the boat, seated her on a board which lay across the bottom, and taking up the pole, directed John to step on board. He then pushed the boat across the stream and entered the little inlet where they had been the previous night.

"Here we is," said Neddy, "as safe as a rat in his hole. Now, I'll jes go up to de hous and see 't all's right afore you go up."

So he clambered up the bank, fastened the boat-chain to the same little tree where it had been the previous night, and started toward the deserted house, leaving the fugitives in the boat.

He walked slowly toward the house. Everything seemed silent and dreary. The moon was just visible as it peeped faintly over the hill to the west. The great trees of the forest, with their outstretched arms, looked as though they stood listening and waiting for something from the great Unknown. The plaintive voice of the katydids served only to deepen the awful and majestic silence. He felt strangely uneasy, and oppressed with some unknown and undefinable dread, but still moved forward. Reaching the door of the house he pushed it open, and stepping inside, took some matches from his pocket for the purpose of lighting the candle left there on the previous night.

Just at this moment there arose from the direction of the boat a shriek so wild, so despairing, so expressive of the extremest mortal agony, that it froze his very blood and transfixed him, horror-stricken, on the spot where he was standing.

CHAPTER IX.
THE HUNTERS AND THEIR PREY.

"Like a lion growling low--
Like a night-storm rising slow--
Like the tread of unseen foe."

THE tavern, already referred to, at which the slave-hunters had put up, was but a few hundred yards from the Maryland line. In their approach to Brown's they would, in all probability, cross the Octorara at Carter's, and proceed thence by the way with which our readers are already familiar.

To reach Carter's they had their choice of two different routes, both of which, however, converged into one at Buckingham school-house, a point about half a mile west of the former place, and on the opposite side of the creek. From the school-house the approach to Carter's was through a wood, which on the one side reached down to the dam, some distance below the deserted house. From this road to the dam, through the wood, the distance was not over two hundred yards, while the deserted house was distant more than half a mile.

Davy McCann, who was well and accurately informed in relation to their intended movements, determined to watch them closely. He believed that for the present they were completely foiled by the plan which had been put into execution. Long experience, however, had taught him to calculate for every contingency, and to watch closely each turn of events, realizing in the meantime that eternal vigilance was the price of liberty. Accordingly, as evening approached, he determined to take his stand at Buckingham school-house and await the coming of the slave-hunters who, he felt sure, would pass there soon after dark.

So, crossing over wood and field, he reached the spot just as the shades of night were settling down, and taking his seat in a clump of bushes near the road-side, awaited their coming.

Davy did not have to wait long. He was just comfortably seated and had provided himself with a huge quid of tobacco, which he was masticating with his usual energy, when a low rumbling sound admonished him that a vehicle was approaching. It was somewhat earlier than he had expected the slave-hunters, but peering through the darkness he saw a covered wagon with two horses attached, preceded by two men on horseback, approaching. There could be no mistake about their identity; they answered the exact description he had receive of the party in search of John and Mary, and besides, this road was but little traveled, and the party evidently were strangers. He made no doubt that they were going direct to Brown's, and as soon as they had passed his place of concealment, started quietly and cautiously through the wood, keeping them in sight.

What was his utter astonishment to see the whole party, shortly after they had passed the school-house, leave the public road and turn into the wood in the direction of Carter's dam.

At first he conjectured they did this for the purpose of concealing themselves until later in the evening, not desiring to approach Brown's until the family had gone to bed.

This theory, however, soon vanished, for, approaching as near as possible without danger of detection, he saw the wagon stop about fifty yards from the road, while the two men on horseback dismounted and tied their horses. Three persons then emerged from the wagon, and the horses attached to it were also tied to a tree. A short and hurried consultation was had, which resulted in four of them, one being evidently a guide, striking off rapidly in the direction of the dam, while one remained in charge of the horse and wagon.

Davy for a moment was staggered. This turn of affairs was so utterly unexpected, and at first so incomprehensible, that he was completely at fault. But his mind, trained to meet desperate emergencies, quickly rallied, and the true state of affairs flashed like lightning upon him. There was treason somewhere, and the kidnappers, under the direction of a guide, were on their way to capture the fugitives at the deserted house!

His mind was made up instantly. These men could not be back in much less than two hours. The way was rough and difficult to travel, and the fugitives in all probability would make some defense. If they were overcome, the task of bringing them to this point would be a tedious one. Carter's was but half a mile distant and Brown's three-fourths of a mile farther on. From both these places he could have aid before the return of the kidnappers, sufficient to overcome them and rescue the fugitives.

So he quietly retreated some distance, and then started off rapidly in the direction of Carter's mill.

He was a swift mover and a rapid thinker, and all his energies were now fully aroused. Before he had reached the ford at Carter's he had decided what course to pursue. All the force that could be rallied must be brought to the point where the slave-hunters would bring their prey. It would be useless to attempt to follow them to the deserted house, as in this way they might be missed and make their escape. To bring a force sufficient to overcome them and rescue the fugitives, when they reached the point where the horses and wagon were standing, was now Davy's supreme aim; to this he determined to bend all his energies.

Billy Brown sat by his kitchen fire, after the departure of Neddy and the fugitives, with much less than his usual calmness. He felt, of course, convinced that the kidnappers would be foiled, and yet he could not dispel a vague uneasiness that something might yet happen to place the fugitives in their power. He expected their arrival some time during the evening, but could scarcely resist a desire to walk out on the road they would approach and catch the earliest glimpse of them. Indeed, something might have happened to change their plans, and possibly they would not come at all. Carter's might know something about it and neglect to send him word that night, and he felt a strong desire to walk down and see. But Margaret and Martha would be alone if he went, and that would not do at such a time. So he contented himself arranging and disarranging the fire, with the great kitchen tongs, until a quiet knock was heard at the door; and in answer to an invitation to come in, Joe Simmons entered, carrying his double-barreled gun.

Joe, as we have before stated, was always heartily welcome at Brown's, being a favorite with all the family; and to-night he was greeted with more than customary warmth; so true it is that the heart nestles more closely to tried friends when care and trouble gather around us.

He was scarcely seated by the kitchen fire when Billy gave him a brief statement of the condition of affairs, adding:

"Joe, I guess I'll walk down toward Carter's; mebby they've heerd sumthin' new about it; will thee stay and take care of the wimmen?"

"Yes, I'll do the best I kin. Peggy didn't yust to be very skeery, tho', but she looks a little oneasy to-night."

Margaret was laboring under considerable excitement, but she kept it down and said nothing.

Billy lost no time in starting, and walked rapidly in the direction of Carter's mill. Something seemed to impel him forward. Reaching the top of the hill he heard the footsteps of the boys along the edge of the wood, and stopped a moment until they came up.

"Well," inquired he, "how did Neddy get across?"

"Don't know," was the answer. "He started us off as soon as the boat was up, and we thought we heard somebody a-screamin' over there just now; sumthin' must be wrong."

"I'm goin' down to Carter's, mebby they know sumthin'; come along."

In a few minutes they reached the mill, just as Davy McCann and Bristow Wilson were coming out at the door.

"Davy, 's that thee--what's the matter?"

"Matter enuff, I was just cummin after ye; follow me now and ask no questions."

The whole party implicitly obeyed; after they had gone a short distance Davy stopped suddenly:

"Bristow, have ye a small rope in the house?"

"Yes, I have, an' it's a mighty good one."

"Go in an' git it as quick as you kin."

Bristow's house was on the way from the mill to the foot-log, over which they would cross the creek. He entered, and in a few minutes re-appeared with a coil of stout rope.

"Now," said Davy, we must stir ourselves, I'll go ahead; let no man speak a word."

Over the creek, up the path by the side of the road, and through the wood they followed him in Indian file, until within about a hundred yards of where he had seen the slave-hunters leave their wagon and horses, when he stopped.

After briefly explaining the situation he said: There's but one man there now, but he must be taken by surprise; he's arm'd and might give ye trouble. We must surprise him and tie him, so as to git him out uv the way when the rest comes up. You stay here and don't move, while I slip up and see what he's doin'."

So Davy glided off through the darkness, so quiet and cat-like that even those left behind could scarcely see his movements. In a few minutes he returned.

"He's sittin' with his back against a small tree. I'll slip up and seize him; but some one must be close behind to help me. We must not let him holler. Who'll go with me?"

"I'll go," said Bristow, quickly; "here, Billy take the rope."

"I'll go, too," said Billy.

"No, let Bristow come alone, we'll have plenty of work for ye all after a bit."

The slave-hunter was sitting on the ground with his back against a small tree, and his eye anxiously strained in the direction his companions had gone. In his right hand he held a small single-barreled pistol, more because he had brought it along, than from any expectation that it would be necessary to use it. Suddenly a stinging blow fell on his arm, the pistol dropped from his grasp, and at the same moment he was hurled forward to the ground, face downward. Attempting to recover himself, he found that he was in the hands of two powerful men, and was informed, in no very gentle terms, that if he offered any further resistance, or attempted to scream or call for help, the pistol that had just fallen from his hands would be used to blow out his brains.

This information had the desired effect, and no further resistance was offered. Billy came up with the rope, and the man was securely tied and lifted into the wagon.

Bristow could not resist an inward chuckle. "Billy," said he, heartily, "that's what would be call'd a good job;" and his powerful frame shook with suppressed laughter.

"Never mind," said Davy, "we've a heap to do yet. They'll soon be here, I think. Now we'll leave the horses and wagon jest as they are, so's if they see 'em they'll think all's right. You jes slip into that bunch of laurels, all of ye. I'll stay here an' watch, an' if this feller shows any signs of makin' a fuss, I'll give him the medasun he brot along for us, with this." He held up the pistol, and his eyes gleamed with a dangerous fire.

So, into the bunch of laurels the four, Bristow, Billy and the two boys, went and seated themselves as comfortably as they could, while Davy kept a lookout for the approaching slave-hunters, and an eye on the captive in the wagon.

When the party of kidnappers, guided by Sam Doane, as our readers have already suspected, left their horses and wagon in the woods they proceeded as rapidly as possible toward the deserted house. Sam had learned, by means that our readers will find out by and by, of the plan of secreting the fugitives, and resolved at once to take advantage of it. He had conveyed information to the hunters in the morning, and it was in consequence of this that they started so early, in order, if possible, to reach the vicinity of the house and conceal themselves before the arrival of the fugitives.

In pursuance of this plan they moved rapidly up the right bank of the creek, under the guidance of Sam, who knew the place well, and secreted themselves in the bushes at the very point where Neddy landed with the boat, as we have already learned.

Their design had been, at first, to let the whole party land and then overpower them, tie Neddy, leave him in the deserted house, and take the fugitives down in a boat to a point near where they had left the team; but when he got out of the boat and started toward the house alone, they saw their difficulties much lessened. Waiting until he had reached the house, two of them stepped forward, sprang into the boat and with drawn pistols ordered the fugitives to utter not a word.

John felt impelled to leap into the stream, but the sight of the pistols quieted him, and he relapsed into his customary stolidity.

Not so, however, with Mary. The sight of her master, appearing so suddenly, so unexpectedly and so incomprehensibly, with the conviction that she and her child were again hopelessly in his power, brought to her mind so forcibly the utter wretchedness of her situation that she uttered the despairing shriek that had so startled Neddy, and fell on the bottom of the boat in a dead swoon.

The slave-catchers feeling that no time was to be lost, immediately placed a pair of handcuffs on John, who made no resistance, laid the woman in one end of the boat, seated Charlie, who was terror-stricken and bewildered, by her side, and pushed rapidly down the stream.

Their great object now was to make the best possible time. If they could reach the wagon with their captives and get fairly started on the road home before the neighborhood was alarmed, there would be no danger. But of this they did not feel sure. Neddy would be certain to take some action to intercept them, as soon as he discovered what had occurred, and they felt that every moment was of the utmost importance.

So they made with all possible speed for the point on the dam nearest the place their wagon and horses had been left, and having reached it, jumped out on the bank, which was low there, and prepared to move as rapidly as possible through the wood.

Mary, who had recovered consciousness, stepped slowly and wearily from the boat, while one of the kidnappers took Charlie in his arms and set him on shore. They then discussed the propriety of tying her hands before starting, but one more sagacious than the rest said:

"No use in tyin' the wench, she'll not run away while we've got the young un."

So they started forward, the guide in advance; John, who was handcuffed, followed; next came his owner, carrying Charlie, then Mary, while the two remaining slave-catchers brought up the rear.

The prediction in regard to Mary proved true. She followed her master, who bore the boy in his arms, without making any attempt to escape.

Davy's quick ear detected their approach in the distance. He glided silently in that direction, and returning, whispered:

"Keep still as death. They'll pass close by where we are. Brister and Billy take the two hindmost men. You boys, the one ahead, and I'll tackle the fellow that's carryin' the boy. I'll yell; it'll skeer 'em, an' they'll be easier trounced."

On they came, with Sam Doan at their head. Little did they think that strong arms and beating hearts were close by, ready to hurl them to the earth.

They moved more slowly as they neared the wagon, and paused within a few rods of the clump of laurels where the rescuers were concealed. Just at this moment Davy uttered one of the most unearthly yells that ever resounded in human ears and springing forward with the agility of a panther grappled the man who held the boy in his arms. Bristow and Billy each went for his man, and in less time than it takes to relate it, were engaged in a fierce struggle. Sam Doan was for a moment bewildered, but quickly recovering, before the boys could reach him, started through the woods with the fleetness of a deer. They attempted pursuit but were recalled by Davy, who, never losing his presence of mind, understood that nothing more was to be apprehended from Sam, while the boys were badly needed where the contest was now raging in full fury.

When the man who carried Charlie realized that they were attacked, he dropped him and closed with his assailant. The boy was slightly hurt and badly scared, and uttered a suppressed scream. In a moment his mother, who, until now, scarcely realized the situation, grasped him in her arms--one thought filling her mind--one purpose in her soul. He was hers again, and there was hope. How much, she did not know--she did not care. She was free again, her child was in her arms, and through the deep, dark wood, with the swiftness of thought she fled. Onward--onward--onward. Like the mother who scaled the mountain top--hitherto inaccessible to human feet--to bring back her child, which the eagle had borne to his eyrie, on she went. No weakness or weariness oppress her now. Strength and activity are hers in measureless profusion. The boy does not feel to her a feather's weight, and her feet scarcely seem to touch the earth. That mysterious store-house of nature, in which latent strength and energy are laid away for great occasions-- and for them alone--is unlocked and its treasures are hers. On--on--on--till she sees the waters glistening through the trees and knows it is the Octorara. Down beside the stream, without abating her speed, until she reaches a foot-log which crosses the creek. Her mind is clear--clear as her purpose is strong. She recognizes the place as that where she had crossed with Davy, when on the road to Brown's. Her heart gives a great throb of joy, for now she knows the way to a place of comparative safety. Across the log, high and narrow though it was, with Charlie in her arms, she went. Her footsteps never faltered, her purpose never flagged. Across the creek and over the route that Davy had taken her and John, she fled. Up the hill from Carter's, with the boy pressed closely to her bosom, she goes. Her shawl has been torn from her shoulders and is hanging on the bushes in the dark wood behind. Charlie's cloak has been rent, and is in fragments, but he is unhurt, and out of the hands of the slave hunters. That thought fills her soul and she cares not for shawl or cloak. She has reached the top of the hill, and now, down another, and she will soon be at Brown's.

Her speed lessens as she nears the house, her limbs tremble, her breath grows thick and short, but still she presses on--still she clasps the boy to her heart. The yard-gate is reached, and pushing it open, she sees, through the window by the firelight, Margaret Brown seated at the kitchen fire. One more effort, and all will be well. Gathering up every energy she throws open the door and with eyes distended, great clusters of foam gathered about her mouth, and blood streaming from her nostrils, totters feebly forward, and placing the boy in Margaret's arms, exclaims:

"Take him--oh God! Missus--take him," and fell senseless to the floor.

CHAPTER X.
FOILED.

"He who treads profanely on the scroll of law and creed,
In the depth of God's great goodness shall find mercy in his need;
But woe to him who crushes the SOUL with chain and rod,
And herds with lower natures the awful form of God."

WHEN Jem Body parted with Neddy and Bristow Wilson at the mill, he made his way home with all possible speed. He never missed a dancing party among the colored people, when it was possible to attend, and had pledged his word to be present at this one. He regretted the necessity which forced him to disregard the request of these men, for Jem was true to his race, and would gladly have rendered assistance to the fugitives; but he could not think of absenting himself on this occasion, and to attend to both was simply impossible.

Besides, he had an additional motive for wishing to be present at the party. He had some time previously made the acquaintance of a dusky damsel, several shades lighter than himself, whose sprightly ways and pleasing looks had quite captivated him, and having seen her "home from meetin' " on the previous Sunday evening, she had informed him that she would, beyond a doubt, be at the party that night. Under such circumstances it was out of the question for Jem to permit anything to prevent his attendance.

On his way home he revolved the subject in his mind, and repeated to himself, audibly, the importance of keeping what he had heard a profound secret. "Dat I won't tell nobody, be derned if I do, not even de gal," was his concluding remark.

The house, occupied by a negro named Porter, at which the party was held, was a small log building, such as was usual for colored people to occupy in those days, and was located some distance north of where Jem lived, and about two miles from the deserted house. To this place Jem repaired, after he had reached home and made such arrangements as were necessary for an early departure with his team in the morning.

When he reached the party it was quite late, and the dancing had been for some time in progress. The house was crowded, and in order to make room for the dancers, a number remained outside and enjoyed the scene by looking through the windows. Of the lookers-on, several were white persons, whom curiosity had brought to the place in order to see the dancing, for in this amusement the negroes were noted for great proficiency.

Jem entered with zest into the exercises of the evening, and for a while forgot all about the conversation at the mill. His favorite girl was there, as she had promised to be, and the pleasure of the dance and her society drove all other thoughts from his mind.

It was customary at such gatherings, at that time, to have a plentiful supply of whisky on hand, and this one was no exception to the rule. It was usually secreted in some place out of doors, and there the male portion of the dancers repaired occasionally, and semi-occasionally, to refresh themselves.

On the evening in question two half-gallon jugs filled with "rye" had been hidden in a small stable near the house, and a few favorites of the host, among whom were Jem Body, informed of it. They commenced by going out slyly and partaking moderately of the "critter," but soon became less careful and more demonstrative, as they began to feel its effects. Jem was not a habitual drinker, but on such occasions, when surrounded by boon companions, was apt to get a little "mellow," and was then, like most other men, more than usually communicative.

After several potations the secret he had learned from Neddy and Bristow Wilson began to oppress him, and he commenced throwing out vague hints that he "know'd sumthin', but there wasn't enny body goin' to find it out--not enny."

After a few more drinks Jem began to inform his companions, as they gathered round the jugs which were rapidly being emptied, that he was "jest de boy to go thro' a kidnapper," adding, "and dey's about too, boys, I tell you dey is."

Now Sam Doan, who was coaling in the neighborhood, was one among the white people who were looking on at the dance. In fact, he had come for the express purpose of ascertaining, if possible, whether any of the negroes in

92

the neighborhood knew of the presence of the fugitives at Brown's, and whether there was any project on hand to remove them. Sam was in communication with the slave-hunters, and having been promised a large reward if they were successful, he was on the alert to detect any scheme that would frustrate their plans.

Understanding well the virtue of whisky in obtaining secrets from these people, he had provided himself with a bottle, which he had concealed some distance from the house, intending to use it when the proper time arrived.

The exclamation of Jem in regard to kidnappers, which was made in a loud voice, reached his ear and excited his curiosity. He determined to keep a sharp lookout.

After some time Jem Body, who now saw the world and its inhabitants through an entirely different medium from what he had some hours previously, concluded that he must impart the grand secret to a few of his companions. Taking them out some distance from the house, he told them of the whereabouts of the fugitives and the plan on foot to avoid the slave-catchers. In his enthusiasm he claimed to have originated the idea of conveying them to the deserted house, and assured his hearers that "De debbil himself couldn't find 'em dar." All this was done amid profuse promises on the part of those who received the information that they "never would tell a livin' critter."

Sam was on the alert, and, though he heard nothing, was sure from Jem's manner and his previous declarations that he was communicating something in relation to the fugitives.

Among those who formed the group to whom Jem imparted his secret was one that Sam knew to be unusually fond of liquor, having frequently furnished him with that beverage on former occasions when he desired to be initiated into his good graces; from him he determined to find out what Jem had said.

Watching his opportunity when no one was nigh, he slipped up and whispered:

"Wouldn't ye like to have a little reel good stuff."

"Yes, sah, I wud indeed. Has ye got sum?"

"Jes go out behint that big oak tree off yander, an' wait till I cum."

So off went the thirsty gentleman of color, and the wary old collier soon followed. When he reached the tree indicated he drew forth from a little hollow, close beside the tree, a quart bottle filled with whisky, where it lay covered with leaves.

Seating themselves on the ground the two proceeded to test the quality of the liquor. The negro pronounced it "fust rate," and indulged in deep potations, while Sam tasted it with great caution, but was equally profuse in its praises. Gradually the latter drew the conversation on to the desired subject, and succeeded in eliciting from his companion the whole story that Jem had imparted.

He saw at once the great importance of prompt action, and after making a few remarks on other subjects declared that he must "go over and see to the pits," as he had almost forgotten them. He left, however, what remained of the liquor with his colored friend, telling him he was welcome to it all.

Sam proceeded at once to the coaling ground, and after examining his pits, left them in charge of his assistant, while he hastened to inform the slave-catchers, who were at the tavern before referred to, of the contemplated movement that night. After a long conversation, the plan already known to our readers was agreed upon, and Sam returned with the promise to meet them near Buckingham schoolhouse, on the next evening at dark, which he did. He was exceedingly cautious in his movements, fearing vengeance from the colored people, if detected. This was the reason of his precipitate flight when the party were attacked, as has been before described.

Neddy Johnson remained for some moments riveted to the spot when he heard the appalling shriek uttered by Mary upon discovering that she was again in the hands of her master. He was astounded, bewildered and, for a moment, terrified. He had felt so perfectly secure that the idea of detection or discovery never entered his mind. The knowledge that something of that kind had happened came upon him like a clap of thunder from a clear sky.

Recovering himself, he proceeded cautiously toward the place where he had left the boat and its occupants, and on reaching it discovered that they were gone. Peering through the darkness, he saw the boat moving rapidly down the dam, and already some distance away; while the forms of several men could be discerned on board.

Neddy's mind did not act rapidly; but his judgment was generally correct. Remembering the conversation with Jem Body, and the terrible fright indicated by Mary's shriek, he came to the conclusion that these were the slave-catchers, and that by some means they had become possessed of the information communicated to Jem, which had enabled them thus to outwit and circumvent the fugitives and their friends.

But he did not give up to despair. He promptly resolved to follow them and take advantage of the first opportunity, should any occur, to recover the runaways.

In pursuance of this, he proceeded down the bank of the stream as rapidly as possible; but the way being rough and difficult, his progress was necessarily slow. Emerging at length from the woods, he reached an open field, and after passing this and groping for a short distance through another wood, came upon the boat where it had been left by the slave-catchers when they landed with their captives. This was a poser, and he cudgeled his brain in vain to find a satisfactory solution of it. It never occurred to him that they had left a team near the public road, and that this was the nearest point from which to reach it. While he was making fruitless efforts to see through the difficulty, the yell of Davy McCann, the signal for the attack on the slave-catchers, resounded in his ears and decided his course. With scarcely any conception of what it meant, but feeling sure it was something connected with the fugitives and their captors, he started in that direction at full speed.

When Davy McCann recalled Henry Brown and Samuel Weaver from their pursuit of Sam Doan, he began to feel that he needed all the aid he could muster. He had, in fact, attacked the most formidable man of the crowd, and though he retained in a remarkable degree the strength and agility that had characterized him in early life, yet age had impaired his power of endurance to a greater extent than he was willing to admit. His opponent was a man of iron frame, in the prime of life, possessing coolness and courage as well as great activity. Though disconcerted at first by the suddenness of the attack, he speedily recovered; and had not Davy had the presence of mind to call back the boys to his aid, he would undoubtedly have come out second best in the struggle. As it was, with their aid the man was borne slowly to the ground, and preparations made to tie him.

Billy Brown and Bristow Wilson had each got the better of his man without much difficulty, but neither could secure them without help, and it was unsafe to let them go; so they had to remain passive spectators of Davy's struggle with his formidable opponent, without having it in their power to render any assistance.

In the meantime, the man who had been tied and placed in the wagon before the arrival of the fugitives and their captors, had not been by any means a quiet spectator of the affair. From the moment of the attack on his comrades, he had been using his utmost efforts to slip the rope with which his hands were tied; and about the time Davy and the boys had fairly overcome their man, he succeeded. This accomplished, the rest was short work; taking out his pocket-knife, which his captors had left untouched, he quickly cut the cords which bound him, and leaping from the wagon, rushed to the assistance of his friends.

Bristow Wilson, who had been watching with unconcealed anxiety the progress of the affair, saw this new feature in the struggle, and felt that the time for decisive action had come. Leaving his man on the ground, he sprang like a tiger toward the released captive, and quick as lightning dealt him a crushing blow which sent him quivering to the earth.

In the meantime the man he had left, who was yet unhurt, sprang to his feet and was in the act of drawing a pistol, which had remained concealed about his person, when a blow dealt by some unseen hand laid him prostrate and senseless on the ground.

This was Neddy, who, coming up unnoticed, had taken in the situation at a glance, and being in no humor for half-way measures, had struck him with all the force he could command.

This decided the contest; the three men were tied, and the one who had given Davy so much trouble had the hand-cuffs he had put on John placed on his own wrists. He took it coolly, and said nothing.

96

John had remained a passive spectator of the affair, neither endeavoring to escape nor offering to assist. He could not have rendered much assistance, being hand-cuffed, but he showed no disposition to try. He manifested the same stolid indifference that had characterized him ever since his first appearance in the neighborhood.

"Where's Mary?" said Billy Brown, when the men were securely tied.

"She's dun gon'," said John, "she went off through de woods, takin' de young un."

"Never mind," said Bristow, "she'll take care of herself. We'll find her to-morrow if we don't to-night. What'll we do with these rascals?"

That was indeed the important question. They felt as though an elephant was on their hands, which they scarcely knew how to dispose of.

"Sarch 'em," said Billy Brown, "the first thing and see if they've got enny more pistols."

This suggestion was adopted, and all were found to have arms. The suddenness of the attack had prevented them from being brought into use.

These were placed in the hands of Neddy and the two boys to guard the prisoners, while the other three retired some distance to consult.

It will be recollected by those whose memories carry them back to that period, that the laws in relation to fugitive slaves were then but imperfectly understood. In fact, there was no very well defined law on the subject. There was a Federal enactment authorizing justices of the peace and other State officers to issue warrants for the arrest of fugitives, and there were State laws to prevent kidnapping, etc., but they were little understood by the common people.

Our friends were well convinced that the slave-catchers would be glad to get back into Maryland without their slaves, if permitted to go, and would not be likely to return. This was, of course, all they could reasonably expect, but their blood was up, and they felt that such an outrage should be punished by law if possible.

After some consultation Davy proposed that they should refer the matter to Grandfather Carter. Everybody relied upon his sound judgment, and he had much experience in public affairs. This all hands agreed to, and Bristow was sent off to obtain his opinion.

Grandfather Carter was in bed, entirely ignorant of the night's performance, when Bristow arrived. The events which had transpired being related to him, he was much surprised, but expressed great satisfaction at the result. He felt as the rest did, that it would be very gratifying to have the kidnappers punished by law, but doubted the propriety of retaining them. His experience at court in contests with slave-holders had made him wary of entering them, and when the main point, the escape of the slaves, could be secured without it, he preferred to avoid them.

"Bristow," said he, "if we prosecute them the chances are that we will lose the suit, and in the end they'll be purty sure to git the slaves. They'd better let the fellows go; they're frighten'd now, and won't come back soon. In the meantime the blacks can get to a place of safety."

This advice agreed with the conclusion previously arrived at, and Bristow hastened to return and make it known to his comrades. They at once prepared to put it in execution.

Bristow was spokesman for the party. Stepping forward with an unaffected dignity that never forsook him, and a force and effect that always accompanied his words, he told the slave-hunters of the conclusion that had been arrived at. He informed them if they would go home and promise not to return in search of these people, they would be set at liberty; otherwise they would be prosecuted for kidnapping.

He did not expect their promise to be of much value, but thought he might as well exact it, as it could do no harm; he had far more faith in their being deterred by the wholesome fear that the occurrences of the night had inspired.

They hesitated about promising, but finally agreed to do so. The two who had come on horseback were then released and started off. After some time the one who had been handcuffed was placed in the wagon, and his companion untied. These were also soon started off, and the victors remained alone on the ground.

It was now well nigh midnight. The moon, had long since disappeared. The little stars looked down silently through the tops of the forest trees, unmindful of the fierce struggle they had just witnessed. The dull roar of Carter's dam was the only sound that disturbed the stillness of the night.

The parties slowly separated; Davy McCann going alone toward his home, while the rest started in the direction of Carter's. Previous to leaving Davy informed the rest that he would see them on the next evening.

It was agreed that John should go back to Brown's, until the whereabouts of Mary was discovered; when measures must be taken to have them at once removed.

The impression with all hands was that she must have taken refuge at some house in the neighborhood, and would be discovered in the morning.

"Ging-god," said Neddy, "Dat woman beats all ever I seed. She's wuth half a dozen sich fellows as her man."

John was walking behind, but did not notice the remark; all who heard felt its truth.

Bristow thought it possible that she had stopped at his house, which was on the road she had most probably taken. When they reached it he inquired, but no one had been there.

Billy Brown and the boys hurried home. They knew the family would be uneasy at their prolonged absence, and thought it quite possible that Mary had reached there. On their arrival they found this conjecture correct; Mary was there, and the circumstances of her arrival were related by Margaret and Joe.

They had brought down a bed into the parlor and kindled a wood fire there. Mary was laid on the bed, and after having some French brandy forced into her mouth, partially recovered. She was much agitated though, and started up wildly every few minutes, calling for Charlie, and manifesting what Margaret called "flightiness." Her nervous system had evidently received a severe shock.

Billy related what had happened during the night, and all listened with the deepest attention. A feeling of great relief showed itself on Margaret's face when he concluded by expressing his conviction that there was no danger of the slave-catchers returning.

The family then, with the exception of Margaret, retired to bed; she was not willing to leave Mary in her present condition without some one to watch at her bedside; and there was no one suitable for the task but herself.

The woman was restless and feverish through the night, and showed unmistakable symptoms of delirium. Margaret was a good deal alarmed, and told her husband, when he came down-stairs in the morning, that he had better go for Doctor King without delay.

CHAPTER XI.
DOCTOR KING.

'The violet droops its soft and bashful brow,
But from its heart sweet incense fills the air--
So rich within--so pure without--art thou,
With modest mein and soul of virtue rare."

No man ever lived in the section of country where the events we have been describing transpired, more generally beloved and universally respected than Doctor Jeremiah King. At the period to which we refer, he resided in Little Britain township, Lancaster county, near the village now known as Oak Hill, but which at that time went by the name of "Hill Tavern," a tavern, store and one or two other houses comprising the settlement.

A short distance from here was the residence of Dr. King. The house was a small log building nearly surrounded by woods, and some distance from the public road, from which it was approached by a foot-path. The doctor at this time was probably about 40 years of age, and had for many years renounced the practice of medicine, as a business. This was not for want of practice, nor because he lacked skill or knowledge in his profession, for no physician in that neighborhood, however popular, possessed public confidence to so great an extent as he.

He possessed in a remarkable degree the virtues of modesty and conscientiousness, two traits of character perhaps as rare as they are valuable. It is said that he gave as a reason for retiring from the business of his profession, that he distrusted his judgment, that he regarded the administration of remedies for the cure of disease as at best a matter of chance, that while the nature and properties of medicines could be determined, it was difficult--indeed, impossible--to know the effect they would have upon the patient, whose internal condition could never be satisfactorily ascertained. Whether it be true or not that these considerations influenced him to quit the practice of medicine, one thing is certain, he did quit it, after a few years' practice, and never again resumed it.

Being an accomplished chemist, he resolved to turn his knowledge to account in a practical manner, and commenced the manufacture of steel in a small way, from which, with his own hands, he made razors of a very superior quality, known throughout the country as "Dr. King's razors."

Close by his house there flowed a little stream of water, now known as "Pickering's run," and on this he erected a shop where he had bellows, anvil, vise, etc., and a hammer run by water-power. He had also several grindstones, of different degrees of fineness, turned in the same way, and on these his razors were ground.

Here this remarkable man passed his days and earned his livelihood. His razors were sold at fifty cents each--no more, no less. He would not accept more than that under any circumstances--no person could buy, even a hundred of them, at a less rate.

He would take a piece of common iron, convert it into a fine quality of steel, and manufacture it into excellent razors.

He lived in the most economical manner, being a man of exceedingly temperate habits, and dressing himself in the plainest and cheapest style. He usually wore a plain, coarse muslin shirt; a white, slouch hat; pants of homespun, and a red woolen "wammus" or roundabout. When away from home he was mostly on foot, and carried with him a slender steel cane. This was intended as a warning to dogs that he did not desire to enter upon any very intimate relations with them.

But, while Doctor King had retired absolutely from the practice of medicine as a business, he found it extremely difficult to avoid visiting the amilies of many of his friends and acquaintances when they were sick. Many had such unlimited faith in his medical skill that they would have no other physician when it was possible to obtain him; the entreaties of such people, in case of sickness, he found impossible to refuse.

On such occasions they would come prepared to convey him to their homes on horseback, or in a conveyance of some description, bringing him back when the visit was over.

He would never make a charge for these visits, but when money was pressed upon him in return; for such services, would sometimes accept it, always ways with reluctance, and, probably, only because he felt its need.

This peculiarity of the doctor's sometimes induced very miserly persons to send for him, hoping thereby to escape the cost that would otherwise ensue. One instance of the kind was thus related:

A farmer, in good circumstances, living some two or three miles away, had a fall, which injured him considerably. Becoming alarmed, he sent in haste for Doctor King, who came and gave him such relief as was in his power; when he was ready to leave, the farmer said:

"Well, doctor, how much do I owe thee for this visit?"

"Nothing--nothing at all; I say, not anything," replied the doctor.

"That'll never do," said he, "thee can't afford to lose thy time for nothing." Then directing his wife to hand his purse, he carefully selected out an old Spanish "levy," worth twelve and a half cents, and handed it to the doctor, who put it in his pocket, as was his habit, without looking to see what it was.

One of the doctor's eccentricities was his habit of repeating a statement and prefacing the repetition with the phrase, "I say." Sometimes he would repeat this several times, especially when laboring under excitement. Thus, if he had visited some one who was very sick, when asked concerning him, would say:

"He's very poorly--I say, I think he's very poorly," then pausing a moment he would resume, "I say, I think he is."

He was intensely anti-slavery. On this subject alone was he known manifest anger or impatience, in discussion with an opponent. Years after, when the anti-slavery agitation swept over the land, and the vials of pro-slavery wrath were emptied on the heads of all who countenanced "abolitionism," he stood firm and unshaken, among the foremost and most radical of those who held fast to the doctrine that all men were entitled to "life, liberty and the pursuit of happiness."

No kinder heart, no gentler, purer nature ever came from the Creator's hand. In perfect truth and unswerving honesty the world has probably seen his equal--never his superior.

When Billy Brown had partaken of breakfast, the morning after the adventure with the slave-catchers, he had his horse brought out and geared to the little one-horse dearborn, in which he and Margaret usually went to Friends' meeting, and started off to Doctor King's. Arriving at a point on the public road opposite the house, he hitched the horse to the fence at the road-side, and pursued a narrow path through the woods that led to the doctor's residence.

It was about 8 o'clock, and, as he neared the shop, he heard the click of the tilt-hammer, which told that the doctor was at work. Entering, he found him drawing out a piece of, steel preparatory to making it into razors. He was not observed for a few minutes, and as our readers have, perhaps, a laudable curiosity to learn something of the personal appearance of this remarkable man, who voluntarily abandoned a profession in which he might have risen to eminence, in order to pursue the humble but honorable one in which we find him engaged, we will endeavor to gratify them so far as lies in our power.

As has already been stated, he was about forty years of age, and was rather under the medium height. He was slightly made and somewhat stooped; possessing but a moderate degree of vitality. His head was not large, but well proportioned, the moral and perceptive faculties predominating. His eyes were gray and had an expression of gentleness and kindness rarely equaled. His features were prominent and inclined to sharpness, while his temperament was exceedingly fine, the mental predominating. Added to all, there was an expression of beneficence on his countenance that could not fail to strike the eye of the beholder.

"Good-morning, doctor," said Billy, after having stood watching him for a few minutes.

"Good morning," was the reply, as he looked inquiringly at the visitor. In a moment he stopped the hammer, laid down the tongs which held the steel, and seated himself on a bench near by."

"I've come after thee this morning, doctor," said Billy. "We have a sick woman at our house, and would like thee to come and see her. I've brought the dearborn to take thee and bring thee back."

Here the doctor became nervous and fidgety, got up and walked across the shop, and then sat down again. "Does she seem to be bad; I say, does she seem to be much unwell?"

Billy then told, as briefly as possible, the story of the previous night; the flight of Mary, her arrival at the house and her condition afterward.

Doctor King listened with intense interest. Several times during the recital he arose from his seat, walked across the shop, picked up his hammer and laid it down again, took a small paper of tobacco from his pocket and put into his mouth a piece about the size of a grain of wheat, and after chewing it a moment spit it out, and did many other things which betrayed excitement.

At the conclusion of the story, he said:

"I'll go; I say, I think I'll go. Come up to the house and I'll be ready in a minute."

Billy preferred to remain at the shop and await the doctor's return. In a few minutes he was back, carrying in one hand his steel cane; and the two started up the path which led to the public road.

On the way the doctor asked many questions, and by the time they arrived at Brown's he was familiar with the whole history of John and Mary since their escape into Pennsylvania.

When they arrived they entered the kitchen and found Margaret and Joe Simmons. The boys, who had risen late, were at the shop. Neddy had not made his appearance, and John remained in the garret, preferring to stay there for the day. Frank and Charlie were playing about the kitchen floor. The doctor immediately inquired for Mary.

Margaret informed him that she had grown quieter, and some time since had fallen into an apparently sound sleep. "It's the best thing that could happen her. She mustn't be disturbed. Let her sleep as long as she will; the woman needs sleep."

Looking at Charlie, he inquired if that was the child she had carried in her flight of the previous night, and on being answered in the affirmative, broke out:

"The woman's a heroine; I say, she's a heroine; but they didn't get her; I say, they didn't get her; ha! ha! ha! they must have been disappointed; I say, I think they were badly disappointed;" and he laughed merrily over the discomfiture of the slave-catchers.

Margaret offered to go into the room and see if Mary was still sleeping, but the doctor admonished her that she might disturb her, saying that she would no doubt make herself heard when she awoke. Sleep, he said, was the great remedy for the nervous excitement she had suffered; it was better than all the medicine in the world.

The doctor was then asked to stay for dinner. As Mary might not awaken for some time he consented, and with Joe Simmons and Billy walked out on the porch and sat down. The day was exceedingly fine and he felt in good spirits, exulting greatly over the escape of the runaways from the clutches of the kidnappers. He was especially emphatic in praise of Davy McCann.

"They say a colored man ain't equal to a white man, but Davy can outwit the whole of them; I say, he can outwit them all all. Then there's Bristow Wilson, he's as black as a crow, but we have no better man; everybody trusts him, and he's a man of ability; I say, he's a man of great ability. It's not in the color; I say, it's not the color that makes the man."

He then went into a history of the Constitution of the United States, reciting many of the clauses of that instrument, and contending that slavery was illegal and ought to be immediately abolished. He was familiar with the early history of the country, and held views concerning the unconstitutionality of slavery similar to those advocated years after-ward by leading anti-slavery men.

Margaret, in the meantime, was making preparations for dinner. She had killed a couple of chickens and was cooking them. Knowing that the doctor, who ate little, was very fond of good coffee, she prepared some of that in her best style.

When dinner was nearly ready, she heard a voice in the parlor, and entering, found Mary awake.

"Where's Charlie?" said the woman.

"Charlie's here," said Margaret, cheerily; "come, Charlie, mother wants him," and the little fellow came running in and nestled down close beside her.

"The doctor's here, Mary," said Margaret. "I'll bring him in," and without waiting for an answer she stepped out quickly and informed him that his patient was awake.

Doctor King laid aside his steel cane and walked softly into the parlor. The room had been darkened and Margaret raised the curtains that he might have sufficient light. Taking a chair, he seated himself at the bedside and looked on for some time in silence. Mary did not appear to notice anything except the little boy at her side. Her face rested against his, and her dark, earnest eye glowed with intense feeling. The doctor's kind, artless face was radiant with the unaffected goodness that stirred his inmost heart. More than once he brushed away a tear that had started down his cheek, and did not for a time trust himself to speak. At length he said very gently: "Hold out her hand and let me feel her pulse."

After examining it, he turned to Margaret and remarked:

"She only needs a little rest, there's nothing serious the matter. Her nervous system has received a severe shock, but she'll soon recover. I wouldn't give her any medicine; I say, I think I wouldn't give her any. Maybe she would eat something."

"Mary, will thee have a piece of chicken?" inquired Margaret.

"Yes, Missus, I'll take a little piece."

So a piece of chicken was brought, and some bread. The doctor suggested a cup of coffee, a beverage in which he had great faith.

Mary ate the food and drank the coffee with a good relish. The doctor watched her closely and said:

"Let her have another good sleep and she'll be well; I say, I think she'll be quite well."

The family were then called to dinner, and did ample justice to it. When it was over the doctor intimated that he must leave, and the boys were instructed to gear up the team to convey him back.

Before he started he remarked that the woman should be moved away as soon as possible. She would be able to go by the next evening if nothing unusual happened to her. She ought not, he said, to remain here. Another fright might result much more seriously.

When they were ready to go, Billy said:

"Doctor, how much do we owe thee for this visit?"

"Nothing at all; I say, nothing at all. I wouldn't receive anything for this; I say, I wouldn't receive a cent for it."

This was said in a tone that admitted of no further controversy.

"Well, if thee won't take anything for this, we owe thee for coming here before; take this," said he, placing some silver coin in the doctor's hand.

He looked embarrassed, but put the money in his pocket without examining it.

"Is that right?" said Billy.

"Yes, it's right; I say, it's all right."

"But thee don't look at it. Thee can't tell whether it's all right or not."

"Oh, yes, it's all right, I know by the feel of it; I say, I know by the feel of it."

All present smiled. The doctor looked about nervously, and seemed impatient to be off.

It was now announced that the horse and dearborn were at the door, and with a cheerful farewell and the silent blessing of the whole family the doctor departed.

When he was gone Joe Simmons said:

"There izzent a better man than that ennywhere."

"No," said Margaret, "there ain't many Doctor Kings in the world."

"If he don't get to heaven, Peggy," continued Joe, "there won't be much chance for enny of the rest of us to slip in."

Margaret's face grew serious. This was treating sacred subjects a little lightly, but she replied:

"Indeed, I hope everybody will prepare themselves for that place. It's awful to think of enny one bein' lost."

"How about Sam Doan?" said Joe, laughing.

This was rather a poser. If Margaret hated any living creature it was Sam. Besides, his late actions had made him more odious than ever; still she said:

"Even Sam Doan might get forgiveness if he would ask it sincerely. I hope he will."

"Would you take him into Friends' meetin'?" said Joe.

This was rather too much; the idea of having such a fellow a member of the Society of Friends was so ludicrous that both laughed heartily.

"I think the darkeys 'll give him a 'baptism of fire' of sumthin akin to it, afore long, that 'll do him more good than jinen meetin', and 'll be a good 'eal likelier to make him repent," pursued Joe.

Margaret was silent. Her principles and those of the Society forbade anything like violence; but there was something in the present case that made it feel different to her from any one she had ever met with. She could not find it in her heart to condemn the employment of force under present circumstances.

Joe's prediction proved correct. The next morning the cabin on Sam's coaling ground was found burnt to the ground. A short distance away he was discovered lying helpless, beaten almost to death. During the night a gang of blacks had visited the place, and, infuriated by his treachery, had taken summary vengeance upon him. Except for the interference of one or two, more thoughtful and humane than the rest, he would have been murdered outright. As it was, he barely escaped with his life. Some humane persons near the place cared for him, and he eventually recovered, but left the neighborhood never to return. The perpetrators of the act kept their secret and were never discovered.

Davy McCann came to Brown's on the evening after Doctor King's visit. He had heard of Mary's arrival there and was glad to learn that she was much better. After resting through the afternoon and drinking a cup of strong coffee, she seemed about as well as ever. Davy had found the shawl which Grandfather Carter had presented her and gave it to her. She had lost it in her flight of the night before, and though somewhat torn, it could be easily mended so that it was but little the worse. He had been gathering information respecting the slave-hunters, and found that when they reached Conowingo, on their return, they became very indignant. They swore vengeance against any one from that neighborhood who should ever cross the river, should they know it. They also threatened to return in a few days, but this he did not believe. Still he thought it best that the fugitives should leave at the earliest possible moment, and regarded Doctor King's advice as good. He told Mary to be ready the next evening and he would be there to convey them away. Billy offered to take them some distance in the dearborn, but this offer was positively declined. Davy preferred to travel on foot for many reasons. It was safer; they were not so likely to attract attention; concealment was easier, and he was used to it. He knew all the byepaths and short cuts, that could only be traveled on foot, and he could not think of going in any other way.

The next day Grandfather Carter called. He knew all about what had occurred, and approved of the intended movement. He told Mary not to be afraid. Davy had never yet had a slave captured when under his charge, and would be sure to take them to a place of safety. With this assurance he placed a few pieces of silver in her hand and turned to leave.

"Oh! thank ye, mass'r, thank ye," said the woman, and burst into tears.

"Don't call me master," said the old man sternly, "there is but one to be called Master, and that's the Maker of us all."

Mary looked bewildered, but said nothing. He bade a kind farewell and departed.

In the evening, shortly after dark, Davy made his appearance. John and Mary were seated by the kitchen fire, around which sat the rest of the family. They were prepared to move, and Davy would not even take a seat. He stood by the fire a few minutes, evidently somewhat excited. His mouth was filled with tobacco, which he masticated with all his wonted energy, while his eyes fairly blazed with intense feeling. He was evidently fully aroused and ready for whatever emergency might occur. He said nothing about his proposed destination, but simply remarked that they would travel all night, and lay by in day time. He was acquainted with plenty of stopping-places that were perfectly safe.

Davy had provided himself with a small flask of whisky, to be used in an emergency, in case of excessive fatigue or exposure, and Margaret thought that if they traveled all night they should have something with them to eat. She therefore made up a little roll of provisions wrapped in a newspaper, and tied them up in a cotton handkerchief, which she handed to Davy. They were then ready to leave.

The night was as bright and beautiful as though Nature had designed it especially for the benefit of the wanderers. The moon was in its first quarter, but poured forth a flood of mellow light, while the steady, silent stars beamed down a God-speed to the escaping bondmen. Out into this lovely autumn night--out into the wide, wide world: hope, freedom and happiness beckoning them on; slavery, terror and despair behind--they go. He who tempers the wind to the shorn lamb will protect them.

Joe Simmons remained till they were gone. While they were making ready to start he did not utter a word. His heart was tender as a child's, and he could not trust himself to speak. When they were fairly off, he took up his gun and started for home. Davy returned in a few days and said the fugitives were safe. He gave no further information, nor did any one venture to ask it.

CHAPTER XII.
TIME'S CHANGES.

"The years are viewless angels,
That still go gliding by,
And bear each one a record up
To Him who sits on high."

WE take a long stride forward. Thirty-five years, half the time allotted to human existence, have passed away. Most of those who figured in the events we have been recording have crossed over the dark river, on that voyage from which none have been known to return. In the neighborhood where John and Mary were sheltered and rescued, a new generation has grown up that remembers them not. The Octorara glides onward as sweetly and peacefully as ever; in spring-time the birds fill the deep woods with their strange, sweet music as of yore, while the grandeur of autumn, as as she sits enthroned on the forest-crowned hills, is as enchanting as in days gone by; but those who have been looking with us on these scenes will see them no more forever.

Davy McCann rests in his humble grave, not far from where stood the house in which the later years of his life were passed. In an open common, near the public road, two stones, unhewn, unlettered, mark his resting-place. Around are the graves of a few of his own race--whose youth, like his, was passed in bondage. Here, among those to whom his last efforts were given, the hero reposes. No funeral pageant followed him to his long home. The rich and powerful cared not that the brave old man was dead. A few of his own color and some kind neighbors, who knew his humble worth, stood at the open grave. None others were there.

Away in the land where mothers and their babes were sold at auction, where the clank of the slave-driver's chain and his hoarse and brutal curses mingled with the despairing shrieks of his helpless victims, there was rejoicing. The brave old heart and cunning brain that had so often baffled their schemes were still in death. The slave-hunter felt that the trembling fugitive could no longer be guided by that master-spirit in eluding his grasp.

But on the green hills and in the fertile valleys of the Keystone, where were hidden in quiet nooks and secluded haunts the scarred and hunted

113

bondmen, there were sad and heavy hearts. Slave-mothers wept as they clasped their babes more closely to their bosoms and remembered that the tried and faithful friend, whose rare skill and unfailing courage had so often delivered them from the clutches of the relentless kidnapper, had gone forever from their sight.

Not forever; for when the heavens are rolled together as a scroll, and the oppressor stands with the oppressed before Him who knows the inmost secrets of the heart, and the promised words are spoken: "Inasmuch as ye did it unto the least of one of these, my brethren, ye did it unto me," among the throng of the redeemed will stand that unfailing, constant and unwearied friend, whose life was worn out in the service of the poorest and most helpless of God's creatures.

Grandfather Carter lies buried in the humble little grave-yard at Eastland. At a ripe old age, in possession of all his faculties, he passed away. Stern and unyielding in his convictions, he remained so to his dying hour. He had always felt it to be his duty to maintain a testimony against doctors, lawyers and clergymen. In his last illness friends and relatives besought him to send for a physician. "No," said the stern old man, "I want to die a natural death," and persisted in his refusal to the end.

No stone marks the spot where his ashes repose. No inscription on marble column tells his virtues to the passing multitude; but in the memories of those who knew him well, his sterling integrity, unvarnished but genuine kindness, and great worth, will live while life endures.

In the same enclosure are the graves of Neddy Johnson and Bristow Wilson. Formed by nature for leaders among men, circumstances placed them in a limited sphere of action. With possibilities of greatness the opportunities for distinction did not come to them, but the work their hands found to do was well and fitly performed. Had they belonged to a later generation the possibility might have become a reality; yet their real worth is the same.

The Brown family are scattered. Around the hearthstone no familiar faces gather. At the old kitchen fire-place, where John and Mary sat in the fire-light, only stranger faces can be seen. Billy and Margaret have made their last journey to Eastland. In the plain little meeting-house, the places that knew them so long and well, shall know them no more forever. At a ripe old age, death, the great harvester, gathered them into his garner. Their walk in life was humble and not thornless, but the reward of the good and just is theirs.

Doctor King makes razors no more, but the remembrance of his singular modesty, his unaffected kindness, his sterling honesty and wonderful purity of heart, still lives in the hearts of all who knew and understood his character.

Far away in the valley of Salt Lake Joe Simmons sleeps the sleep that knows no waking. Strange and unaccountable as it may seem, late in life he became a convert to Mormonism. He who had long rejected as unsound the truths of Revelation, as understood by Christians, was led into the mazes of superstition by the cunning devices of the agents of that sect, and followed them to Utah. He never adopted the practice of Polygamy, but died a bachelor, after residing there for many years.

But great events have transpired. The storm that for years was gathering, amidst an agitation rarely equaled for intensity, burst with unequaled fury. Over the land it swept--a hurricane of death and suffering such as the world has seldom seen. When at last its fury was spent, and the gentle sunshine of Peace beamed through the broken war-clouds, the accursed institution of negro slavery was no more. Civilization rejoiced, and casting the slave-whip, and fetters into the dark and bloody ocean of the Past, sang hosannas to Liberty and Peace.

We write not the history of this wonderful period, but only trace the path of individuals to whom its realities were stranger than the most startling pages of romance.

No one has forgotten how slowly and almost imperceptibly the people, the press and the Government reached the conclusion to arm the negroes in defense of the Union.

At first the idea was repugnant to a large majority of the people, but repeated failures, hope deferred and unyielding necessity brought about the result at last. When active hostilities ceased and the mustering out of the Union forces commenced, in the summer of 1865, quite a number of colored troops were in the army, many of whom had rendered valuable and important service to the country.

For some time after the reduction of the army commenced, these troops were stationed in various sections of the extreme Southern States. It was supposed to be necessary to retain a considerable military force for some time in that section, and the negro troops were thought better adapted to the climate than the whites.

One of the finest regiments in the volunteer service was the 33rd U. S. Colored Troops. It was indeed a splendid body of men, mainly recruited in the North. Pennsylvania furnished several companies, recruited from Lancaster, Chester, Philadelphia and adjoining counties.

At the conclusion of active service this regiment was assigned to duty in the department of Florida, then under command of Major-General John Newton.

General Newton, who was an officer of the regular army and a graduate of West Point, declared that there was no better regiment in the service. It was under most excellent discipline, the men obedient, soldierly and prompt in the execution of every order. The non-commissioned officers were superior men--intelligent, dignified and proud of their profession.

They were scattered about in small detachments, at various posts, throughout the State--Tallahasse, Jacksonville, Mellonville, Palatka, Gainesville, Fernandina and St. Augustine.

But in the course of a few months it was thought unnecessary to retain more than the regular troops in the service, and the muster out of the colored regiments began.

Late in the fall the 33rd were collected at Jacksonville, from their various posts, and mustered out of the service of the United States. Most of them took passage from that port to their northern homes; but some, charmed with the glorious winter climate of Florida, determined to remain there until spring. Among these was Sergeant Evans, a non-commissioned officer who had enlisted from Pennsylvania. He had acquired an excellent reputation in the company with which he had served, and had no difficulty whatever in obtaining a recommendation from the officers of the command.

With two of his dusky companions-in-arms he looked around for employment, and at length made application to the quartermaster at that post, who had a large number of men employed in government service.

His application was successful, and for some weeks he was engaged, with his comrades, in performing the not very arduous duties allotted him.

CHAPTER XIII.
KU-KLUX.

"Cruel of heart and strong of arm,
Loud in his sport and keen for spoil,
He little reck'd of good or harm,
Fierce both in mirth and toil;
Yet like a dog could fawn, if need there were;
Speak mildly, when he would, or look in fear."

FLORIDA had many charms for the negro race, especially for those who had been raised in the North. Its genial and lovely climate, which during the winter months, resembled May or early June in the Northern States, seemed an earthly paradise. Instead of the bitter and piercing cold, the driving snow and the long dreary winters of our inhospitable climate, they had almost cloudless skies, a temperature that rarely produced frost, and balmy breezes freighted with rich odors from tropical flowers of unfading beauty. Added to these charms, the forests produced abundance of game, while the rivers teemed with excellent varieties of fish. To the dusky race these were inducements that under ordinary circumstances could scarcely be resisted.

But there were serious drawbacks. To understand these we must glance at the condition of affairs before and after the close of actual hostilities between the Union and rebel forces.

This State was inhabited, before the breaking out of the rebellion, to a great extent by outlaws. Flying from the administration of justice in adjoining States, they sought refuge in this thinly-settled country, where means of concealment were ample and successful pursuit almost impossible. When the war broke out their natural impulses led them to join the rebel forces, which they did mostly as cavalry, forming a kind of irregular force, such as infested Virginia under Mosby and other partisan leaders.

When the war closed these bands of guerrillas were less than ever disposed to adopt the pursuits of civilized life. They had never been accustomed to labor; and now, while the necessity for doing so had been multiplied in consequence of their former slaves obtaining their freedom, their recklessness had been much increased by the circumstances surrounding them during the progress of the war.

But for some time after the close of hostilities they made no marked demonstrations in the way of disturbing the public peace, or defying the laws of the land. In truth, the South was completely subdued. When Lee surrendered to Grant, there were but few, throughout the rebel States, who would not have accepted life and property as the sole condition of entire submission to the Government, and continued obedience to the laws. They felt that in receiving liberty and life they had all they were entitled to, and really more than they deserved.

But soon a reaction set in, and a different state of feeling began to manifest itself. This was greatly assisted by the course of the administration which succeeded that of the lamented Lincoln. The symptoms of sympathy manifested by it toward the late rebels, contributed largely to hasten and strengthen the reaction which followed the first feeling of unconditional submission, and is responsible for much of the mischief that it occasioned.

In Florida the reaction manifested its most malignant forms in an utter disregard for the rights of the negro, and the few original Union men who were scattered through the State. Men, who before the war had been peaceable citizens, did not engage in personal violence against these classes, but winked at it in those who did. Personal injury to a Union man or a negro was rarely, if ever, punished by the civil law, and to evade its execution the most shameless devices were resorted to. This was excused by intelligent and apparently respectable citizens on the plea that their constitutional rights had been trampled upon.

This violent feeling never showed itself toward United States troops. They were treated always with outward respect. Officers, however obnoxious, if clothed in Federal uniform, were safe from insult or violence. So much of the lesson of the war they were not disposed to unlearn.

Early in the winter of 1865-6, General Newton was relieved from the command of the District of Florida, and Col. John T. Sprague, 7th U. S. Infantry, took his place. The volunteer forces were mustered out of service and regular troops placed in their stead. Many of the officers were young men who had seen no actual service in the field, and had but a dim conception of the real purpose and scope of the conflict just closed. Fresh from West Point, where they had imbibed notions at war with the true spirit of democracy, their sympathies were with the aristocracy which had been overthrown by the war, and against the negroes and Union men of the South.

Some of them did not hesitate to express openly their opinion that the war on the part of the government had been clearly wrong, that negro slavery was a good institution and should not have been disturbed, and that the late rebels were an oppressed and sorely-abused people.

These officers, commanding posts where the opportunities for social intercourse were quite limited, naturally sought out those whose tastes, culture and habits sympathized with their own, and by this means their inclination to take part with them was strengthened and intensified.

Col. Sprague, whose head-quarters were at Jacksonville, was an old officer of the regular army, but one who understood his duty and generally performed it in good faith. His orders to his subordinates were of the right character, but they were seldom carried out in their true spirit.

Early in December, the officer in charge of the quartermaster's department received notice that he would soon be required to discharge all civilian employees whose places could be filled by enlisted men. This was done in pursuance of the policy of economy which had been adopted by the Government.

He accordingly notified those in his employ to this effect, among them Sergeant Evans and his two comrades, who had been on duty there for a few weeks.

They began to look about for something to do until spring, when the order for their discharge should come.

One bright sunshiny afternoon, as the employees of the quartermaster's department were standing in front of the building in which the Government stores were kept, in the main street of Jacksonville, they observed a negro crossing the street about fifty yards farther up the river. As he walked across the street, he was met by a white man, who lived a short distance out of the town. As he passed the negro, the latter spoke; but just at that moment something bright gleamed in the sunlight, the black man fell, and his assailant ran about a hundred yards, when he was overtaken and brought back. A crowd collected around the fallen man, among them the surgeon of the post, but no aid could be rendered. He died almost instantly, his throat being cut and the jugular vein severed by a knife in the hands of his assailant. The latter was taken before a civil officer and committed to prison.

Now, it is not singular that an offense of this kind should be committed. Such a thing might occur in almost any community; but the manner in which it was looked upon by the civil authorities is the remarkable part of the affair. At that time the authorities at Washington had directed military commandants not to interfere or take charge of cases of lawlessness, except where the civil power refused or neglected to do it.

In this case the proof of guilt was clear and unquestionable. The man had been seen to strike the blow by, perhaps, fifty people, in broad day-light, in a public street. It was unprovoked, for the negro, as appeared in the evidence, had merely spoken to him, without apparently intending any insult. There could be no doubt of the identity of the guilty party, for some who had seen him do the act had not lost sight of him until brought back, his hands and clothing smeared with blood.

The civil government of Jacksonville summoned a coroner's jury, composed of citizens of the place, and the facts were laid before them. What do you suppose, reader, was their verdict?

It was this: "That deceased came to his death from causes unknown."

This may seem incredible, but it is a stubborn and unvarnished fact. It serves to show what depths of degradation apparently respectable men had reached, through the demoralizing influence of slavery.

When Col. Sprague heard of this he felt outraged, and immediately notified the parties concerned that if the criminal was not punished the case would be taken up by the military authorities. Accordingly he was re-arrested and committed to prison; but the case dragged along so slowly that the commandant was convinced that there was no intention to punish the criminal. Accordingly, he took charge of the case, and had the murderer tried by a military commission. He was found guilty and sentenced to imprisonment for life on the Dry Tortugas.

Some time after this affair occurred, Sergeant Evans informed Captain Brown, the officer by whom he had been employed, that he and his two companions had obtained a situation, and as soon as the order came relieving them they would be ready to go.

"The order is here already, Sergeant, and you will be paid off on Saturday; but where do you go?"

"We have been hired by the railroad agent at Gainesville, to work for the company, cap'n. We'd like to have a line from you recommendin' us, tho'."

"That you shall have," said Captain Brown. "I think I can say you have been faithful and honest men while here."

Sergeant Evans was indeed a remarkable man. Prompt in in the discharge of every duty. Energetic and vigilant in the performance of every trust committed to his care, he could not fail to secure the confidence of his employer. He had enjoyed opportunities of education that did not often fall to the lot of persons of his color and condition in life, and showed a good degree of general intelligence.

"Sergeant," resumed Captain Brown, after handing him what he had written, "ain't it a little risky going out in this State among these rebs? I should think you folks wouldn't be very safe in their hands."

"I dunno," was the reply. "There's a post at Gainesville, and I s'pose they won't disturb us much."

"I hope they won't," was the reply; "but, upon my word, I think you'd be safer in the North."

"I don't want to go North till spring," said the Sergeant. "I made up my mind to spend this winter in Florida, and I'll try to worry it out. I intend to go home in the spring."

"Where is your home?"

"In Philadelphia. I lived there with my mother; my father is dead. I mean to go home in the spring. Mother is anxious for me to come, and I suppose by that time I'll be glad to go."

"Well, I hope you'll have good luck. You'll start for Gainesville on Monday, I suppose?"

"Yes, sir."

So the conversation ended. The men left on the following Monday, and their places as laborers were filled by enlisted men.

The central part of Florida swarms with immense herds of cattle. Sometimes one man owns as many as 20,000 head. Toward the close of the rebellion, the Confederate army depended, in a great measure, for fresh beef, on Florida cattle. In all the other rebel States the supply was well nigh exhausted. Here it was plenty and cheap.

After the conclusion of the war the Federal Government resolved to make its purchases of fresh beef here, for the troops stationed in South Carolina and Georgia. In pursuance of this determination, Capt. Brown was directed to purchase and ship a certain number of beef cattle weekly to Charleston and Savannah. After several shipments the supplies came in slowly, and he found it necessary to go out into the interior of the State to make some arrangements by which larger quantities could be obtained.

Accordingly, on application to Col. Sprague, an order was given him to proceed to Gainesville and other points for that purpose, with directions to the commandant of each post to afford whatever protection might be deemed necessary.

Gainesville, situated on the Fernandina and Cedar Keys railroad, is a pleasant little town of Central Florida, and was at that time a military post, under command of Captain James Cullen, who was stationed there with a detachment of the Seventh U. S. Infantry. Captain Cullen was not a graduate of West Point, but had been appointed from civil life by the first Secretary of War under Lincoln's administration. Like many other appointments that emanated from that source, it was not remarkable for merit, though, to tell the truth, the captain had some good qualities. He was a good-hearted, clever fellow, with plenty of personal courage, having given ample proof of his bravery on several bloody battle-fields of the war. The great trouble with him was that he had not the faintest conception of the underlying principles of the conflict just closed, and possessing but little force of character, yielded to the influences of stronger natures that surrounded him, whatever their tendency might be.

In the present case the social influences of the neighborhood were entirely controlled by unreconstructed rebels--men and women. In the conflict of arms they had failed, and so far they had given up the contest. But they were determined not to be beaten at every point, and their supreme aim now was to control the Federal authorities as much as possible.

Accordingly Captain Cullen was taken possession of by the leading citizens around Gainesville. He was feted and petted by the women, treated with great consideration by the prominent citizens, and made so much of that he really began to think the Southern people were subjected to most unreasonable oppression, and that the "niggers" were totally unfit for any other than the condition from which the war had rescued them--slavery.

Added to this he consumed large quantities of the "ardent," and was very likely to agree in sentiment with those who assisted him in demolishing a bottle or two of "red-eye."

It was late in the evening of a beautiful day in January, 1866, that Captain Brown stepped from the cars at the depot in Gainesville, and inquired of some one standing near the way to the hotel.

The evening was cool for that climate. A short distance away two large fires were burning, around which were gathered quite a number of colored people, employees of the railroad, laughing, talking and enjoying the delightful evening. After learning the direction of the hotel, Captain Brown surveyed these groups, and saw standing among them his old acquaintances of the Thirty-third.

Almost at the same moment he was recognized, and with that respect which is a part of the military discipline, they stepped forward and saluted him. He extended his hand, saying:

"Well, boys, I'm glad to see you. How do you get along here?"

"Right well; don't like it so well tho' as at Jacksonville," said one.

The rest of the negroes, and some white men who were standing near, looked on with astonishment. They had not been accustomed to see a Federal officer speak so cordially to negroes.

"Cap'n," said Sergeant Evans, "if you are going up to the hotel, I'll carry your valise."

So toward the hotel, which was some two hundred yards away, they started; on the way the sergeant took occasion to say:

"Mighty rough place about here, cap'n."

"Do they disturb you any?"

"Yes, cap'n, we have to be very careful. They'd kill a black man as quick as they would a wild turkey."

"Well, I suppose Captain Cullen will give you protection. It's his duty to do that."

"Poor protection we get from him, cap'n, he won't listen to anybody but secesh."

They were now approaching the hotel.

"Where are the head-quarters of the post?" asked Captain Brown.

"Just across there, at the corner of the street, in that big frame building. That is the old court-house."

Captain Brown entered the hotel. The sergeant returned. He had evidently sought an interview for the purpose of giving the captain some idea of the state of affairs around Gainesville.

The hotel was a large and commodious one, capable of accommodating at least a hundred guests. It had been largely patronized by invalids from the North previous to the war, during the winter season. Now, however, it depended mainly on custom from the neighborhood. Quite a large crowd were drinking at the bar, which was in a shed outside of the main building.

Captain Brown entered the hotel, and registering his name, ordered supper, which he was told would be ready in half an hour. He then started over to the head-quarters of the post, to pay his respects to the commander.

Captain Cullen received him with the rough cordiality that was natural to him.

"How are you, old fellow?" said he. "You must make your home with me while you're here; can't put at no hotel; no sir."

"I have already done that, captain, but I will only be here till morning. Do you know any of the large cattle owners in this section?"

"Yes, I do. Devilish good fellows too. There's Johnson, lives about nine miles down south. He's got more cattle than you could shake a stick at. I was at a party at his house last week. Perfect gentleman, he is."

"My business is to make arrangements for purchasing beef cattle for the supply of troops in Charleston and Savannah. Here are my orders."

Captain Cullen looked over the order of Colonel Sprague, and said:

"All right, old fellow. I'll give you anything you need. What'll you want?"

"Nothing but a horse, and perhaps an orderly who knows something of the country. I want to start out to-morrow morning."

"I want to introduce you to some of my acquaintances round here before you leave," said Captain Cullen. "You'll find 'em first-rate kind of people."

"How do they use the darkies since they're free?"

"Better'n they deserve. The niggers are lazy and worthless. They're used better'n they ought to be."

At this juncture there were footsteps in the passage, the door was pushed open a little rudely, and a young man of medium size, dark complexion, with a restless eye and a devil-may-care look, entered the room.

"How are you, Cullen?" said he, boisterously. He had evidently been drinking.

"How are you, McKnight?" said Cullen, shaking his hand with great heartiness. "I'm devilish glad to see you. Here's my friend, Captain Brown. Captain Brown, Mr. McKnight. He's as good a fellow as you ever saw. Was in the rebel army, but aint any the worse for that."

"What branch of the service were you in, Mr. McKnight?" inquired Brown.

"Cavalry, sir."

The two men eyed each other rather inquiringly, neither one seeming quite satisfied with his observations.

"Orderly," said Capt. Cullen to a dirty-looking soldier, who was lounging about the door, "go over to Wilson's and bring a bottle of his best whisky.

Wilson was the man who kept a small grocery in Gainesville. The principal article in his stock of goods was bad whisky.

The orderly soon returned and set down a black bottle, which Capt. Cullen uncorked. "Try that, McKnight," said he, "you're a judge. Here, orderly, bring us something to drink out of."

The soldier, after considerable search, produced a dirty tumbler and two rusty-looking tins.

When the whisky was poured out it smelled like a compound of coal-oil, benzine and turpentine. Cullen and McKnight took long draughts; Brown tasted it carefully.

"Pretty good whisky, that, ain't it, captain?" said Cullen. "How is it, McKnight?"

"Well, I've seen better," was the reply; "but it's a good deal better'n none."

Captain Brown said he must go to supper, which was now ready. Bidding good-evening to the party, he passed over to the hotel.

After partaking of a substantial meal, he talked some ten minutes with the host, who was a Frenchman, and had been there but a short time.

He then passed out on the porch. The night was as beautiful as the imagination could picture. There was no moon, but the stars which studded the heavens so thickly that there scarcely seemed room for them all, shone with a brilliancy that he thought he had never seen equaled. The air was just cool enough to be bracing, without feeling uncomfortable when one was moving about. He walked back and forth enjoying the glorious night.

Suddenly a crowd of some fifteen men came from the direction of the depot, and stopped opposite the hotel, across the street.

They were talking excitedly. Brown walked over near them and tried to learn the subject of their conversation, but they observed him and conversed in whispers. Finally they adjourned to the bar-room where there was another party demolishing "red-eye."

He walked carelessly round near the door and stood admiring the grandeur of the night. After some time one of the party came out carrying with him a load of benzine.

"What's wrong with those fellows?" inquired Brown, carelessly.

"Not much. Nothin' but a nigger bin shot."

"Where?"

"Down at the railroad. Hap'n'd just a bit ago."

"Who shot him?"

"Capt'n McKnight."

"WHAT?"

"Capt'n McKnight, that was in our army. They won't hurt him for it. He's very thick with Cullen, who commands the post here. There's no danger of him being disturbed."

"What was the negro doing?"

"I dun' no."

Captain Brown could scarcely credit the information; but he thought it best to report the matter to the commander of the post. So he crossed over to Cullen's head-quarters and informed him of what he had heard.

1864.   1868.

TIS BUT A CHANGE OF BANNERS.

Photo by Rolfe

CHAPTER XIV.
LOST AND FOUND.

"The land wants such
As dare with rigor execute the laws. * * * * * * *

He's a bad surgeon that for pity spares
The part corrupted till the gangrene spread
And all the body perish: he that's merciful
Unto the bad, is cruel to the good"

CAPTAIN CULLEN was seated alone in his office when Brown entered. The black bottle stood empty on the table. McKnight had gone and carried with him a large portion of its contents. Cullen was more than usually demonstrative.

"Captain," said Brown, when he entered, "it is reported that a negro was shot, at the depot, this evening. Have you heard of it?"

"Yes, I did hear it; but 't ain't true. It's a lie somebody started. They said McKnight shot one; but it's false. He told me it was."

"Did you hear the report before McKnight left here?"

"Yes; some one brought it here, and I asked him.

Brown then related the circumstances under which he had heard the report, and stated his belief that it had some foundation.

"I don't believe it," reiterated Cullen, "but if you want it done I'll send down an orderly to inquire."

"Do you know where McKnight is?"

"No; he went out a while ago; I suppose he'll be in before long. I tell you he's a bully good fellow."

"Well, captain, suppose you send an orderly down to learn the facts of this case. It seems to me that you ought not to be satisfied without knowing the whole truth."

"Well, if you say so, I will; but I'm sure the report's false."

He then called an orderly and directed him to proceed to the depot and make all possible inquiry concerning the affair, and report.

In half an hour he came back and said there was no truth in the rumor. A pistol had been fired off accidentally, but no one had been struck and no damage done.

"Didn't I tell you so?" said Cullen, triumphantly. "You musn't believe what these niggers say. They're the orneriest creatures in creation. Never o't to been set free."

"It was n't a negro that told me, captain," said Brown. "It was a reb, and he rejoiced in the conviction that you would n't have McKnight arrested for shooting one. But I am very glad that the rumor has no foundation. Good-evening."

"Good-evening, captain," said Cullen, "I'll give you whatever you need in the morning."

Brown passed out of the office and directed his steps toward the hotel. A crowd was on the porch, and in the shed which contained the bar there was noise and confusion. Suddenly a thought struck him. It was still possible that the report he had heard was true. His experience in that country had taught him that it was best to believe only what he saw. What if it were true and Sergeant Evans or one of his comrades was the murdered man? They had no friends here, and it was his imperative duty to ascertain the truth. So he turned his footsteps in the direction of the depot, determined to learn the facts for himself, if possible.

When he reached there it seemed silent and deserted. The fires, around which groups of people had been standing early in the evening, had gone out, and only a few embers smouldered there. Several car bodies stood around, some on trucks and some on the ground. In one he espied a glimmering light.

He approached it and rapped against the door. No answer came.

He rapped more vigorously. The light was suddenly extinguished, but still no reply. He called, but no one answered. At length he said: "Is Sergeant Evans in this car?" A voice replied quickly: "No, sah." "Where is he then?" "I dunno, sah."

This was rather unsatisfactory, and it seemed evident that but little information was to be obtained here. He walked down to the railroad track and looked carefully all around. No one could be seen. Finally he discerned a light, some distance away, on the opposite side of the railroad. Toward this he started, and approaching, saw that it came from a small log hut standing in a cluster of trees. As he came near he saw a negro standing by the door.

The latter discerning the United States uniform, went for his fragment of a hat and made a profound bow.

"Well, my man," said Brown, "do you work for the railroad?"

"Yes, sah."

"Where do the men who work here sleep?"

"Dey sleeps in de kaws, cap'n, most uv 'em."

"Do you know Sergeant Evans?"

"Yes, sah, I knows de sargen. He sleep in de kaw."

"Will you come and show me where he is?"

The negro hesitated, and seemed anxious to avoid doing this; but could not positively refuse. At length Brown said:

"Do you know anything about a man being shot here this evening?" He hesitated again, and seemed reluctant to answer.

"You needn't be afraid to tell all you know concerning it," said Captain Brown, at length, perceiving the evident fear under which the man was laboring. "I intend to find out all about it, and mean to have the man who is guilty punished. You shall not be disturbed for telling all you know. If you do not tell you shall be arrested and punished."

"Well, sah, I tells all I knows 'bout it. But if de secesh finds me out dey 'll kill me."

"No danger of that; I 'll see that you are protected. Who was shot?"

"Sargen Evans, cap'n."

"Great God! are you telling the truth?"

"Truth, 'fore God, cap'n. He shot, an' he layin' in de kaw."

"What car is he in? Is he much injured?"

"He 's in de kaw on de wheels, close by de road. De sargen not much hurt; he shot in de hip."

"Come and show me where he is; I must see him."

So, guided by the negro, Brown proceeded to a car body which was standing on a truck about twenty yards from where he had met Sergeant Evans early in the evening. Two boxes, a large and small one, stood by the door of the car, and on these they clambered and rapped against the side. A low voice answered:

"Who dar?"

"De Unyen osfer yere. He want to see de sargen," said the negro.

The door opened cautiously, and a black face peered out.

"Is Sergeant Evans in here?" asked Brown.

"Yes, sah."

"Have you a candle?"

"Yes, sah."

"Light it, I want to come in."

He struck a match and lighted a candle, and Brown entered the car. The negro who had guided him to the place, returned to his cabin.

In one end of the car, stretched on a rude bed, lay Sergeant Evans. Brown approached him.

"Sergeant, what's wrong?"

"I've been shot, cap'n."

"Are you much injured?"

"Not much, I believe. I was struck in the hip by a pistol ball. It is quite painful; but I suppose not dangerous. It has bled a good deal."

This was quite evident; his pantaloons, which were still on, were saturated with blood. On uncovering the wound Brown found it high up on the hip, and looking as though it had been probed.

"Had you a doctor to see you, sergeant?"

"There was one here, cap'n. Some of the rebs brought one who lives about a mile out of town. He examined the wound and said it wasn't of much account. He wanted to take out the ball but couldn't find it. Said he'd be back in the morning."

"Who was it that shot you?"

"A fellow by the name of McKnight; he was in a rebel guerrilla company in the war. I believe they called them 'cavalry' here."

"How did the affair happen? Tell me all about it."

"Well, when I came back from carrying your valise to the hotel, I was standing with the rest around the fire, where I was when you first came here, talking with the boys. Suddenly McKnight and some half dozen others rode up and commenced cursing and swearing at us and calling us all kinds of names. We didn't want to quarrel and said nothing. This seemed to make McKnight still worse, and at last he jumped off his horse and pulling out a revolver swore he would shoot every d----d nigger on the ground. We thought best to leave quietly, I among the rest, as I know him to be a desperate fellow. I started for this car without saying a word, and was within ten feet of it when he fired two shots, one of which struck me, and I fell. He then jumped on his horse and rode away with the rest. The boys helped me into the car, and in the course of an hour the doctor came and asked to see me. When he went away he told me not to let any one know about it."

"Are you sure that it was McKnight that fired at you?"

"Oh, yes; several of them saw him. Every one that was here knows it was him."

"Why didn't you make complaint to the commander of the post?" pursued Brown.

"We did, cap'n; but what's the use of complaining to Cap'n Cullen? George and Sam, the men who were with me at Jacksonville, went up and told him. All he did was to put them in the guard-house. He won't listen to any complaint from our people. He's very thick with McKnight, and the crowd that travel with him, and it's no matter what they do, he'll stand by them."

"You don't mean to say that these men are in the guard-house for simply informing him that McKnight had shot you?"

"Yes I do, cap'n; they are there and for no other reason."

Brown's blood boiled. He was no better or worse than men generally are; but his education had been anti-slavery, and his sympathies were all with the oppressed race. Besides, he thought this action on the part of a Federal officer was an outrage for which there was no excuse.

"Sergeant," said he, "I will go and see the captain myself. The man who shot you must be arrested if he can be found. I will be back here in the morning."

He then bade the wounded man good-night, and directed his footsteps once more toward the quarters of Captain Cullen.

Reaching there he found that officer had retired. The contents of the black bottle had made him drowsy, and he had gone to bed at an unusually early hour.

A soldier was on guard at the door, and he was directed to call the captain. He seemed reluctant to comply; but finally consented. After a long time Cullen dressed himself and came down-stairs.

Captain Brown apologized for his disturbance, and stated his business. He had fully investigated the matter and knew all about the shooting. Cullen expressed his unbelief.

"There is no use in denying and no ground for doubting the fact. I have seen the man who was shot and know him well. He was in my employ at Jacksonville. He is shot and declares that McKnight did it. Captain, you must arrest that man."

"I don't believe McKnight shot him, and I don't want to arrest him. He's a d----d clever fellow and belongs to one of the best families in this neighborhood."

"I don't care what family he belongs to or who he is. He must be arrested and placed under guard to await Colonel Sprague's order. There is no civil authority in this county, and if there were it would be worthless. It is not worth while to waste words about the matter, but if you don't do it I'll return to Jacksonville in the morning and report the whole affair to Colonel Sprague."

This remark had the desired effect. Much as Cullen was disinclined to arrest his associate, he disliked still more to incur the displeasure of Colonel Sprague who, he knew, was not very friendly to him at best.

"Well," said he, "I suppose there is no other way. Where is McKnight?"

"I suppose he is somewhere about the hotel."

"Orderly, go and tell Sergeant Beam to report here with a file of men immediately."

This order was obeyed, and in a short time the officer and men made their appearance. The sergeant was a determined-looking fellow, who would be likely to obey orders at all risks.

"Sergeant, do you know McKnight, who is here sometimes?"

"Yes, sir."

"He is said to have shot a man this evening. You must arrest him and put him in the guard-house until further orders. You will find him about the hotel."

"Yes, sir."

He then started. In a short time he returned and said the man could not be found.

"Captain," said Brown, "I'll find him if he is here. Let the sergeant come with me."

This was consented to, somewhat reluctantly, and the party started out.

As they approached the hotel a confused noise of oaths and imprecations were heard in the shed where the bar stood. The soldiers halted, and Brown entered. Amid the crowd of villainous-looking faces he discerned McKnight. Stepping back he told the sergeant to go in and arrest him.

"Forward," said he, and the bayonets glittered in the doorway, the officer in front. Silence fell upon the bewildered crowd, in the midst of which the coarse voice of Sergeant Beam was heard:

"Mr. McKnight, you are arrested, come with me."

The man thus addressed looked up with unconcealed surprise.

"By whose orders?"

"Captain Cullen's, sir."

"Hell and damnation!"

"No words, sir; come along at once."

"What am I arrested for?"

"I dunno, sir."

"Where will you take me to?"

"To the guard-house. COME!"

This was said in a tone that admitted of no delay. McKnight's face was livid with rage; but he dared not show any resistance. So he reluctantly accompanied the resolute sergeant. For a moment the crowd in the bar-room seemed paralyzed. This was something they had not expected. They could scarcely believe that Captain Cullen had ordered the arrest of a man with whom he was so intimate. Finally, after a good deal of consultation together, a part of them started over to see the captain.

Brown sought the porch of the hotel again and walked back and forth, reflecting on the events of the evening.

After some time the crowd which had gone over to Cullen's head-quarters returned. They were citizens of the neighborhood, who usually spent their evenings in Gainesville, and were friends of McKnight.

Approaching Brown, one of them said:

"Captain, thar's no use'n arrestin' McKnight, he didn't shoot anybody. There wasn't anybody shot."

Brown dodged the matter a little at first and said:

"Well, I have nothing to do with that. Captain Cullen is commander of the post."

"But Cullen leaves it all to you. He says he wouldn't have arrested him only for you."

"Captain Cullen is responsible for his own acts."

"Yes, but he's willin' to let him go if you are satisfied. The man's not guilty of anything, and he's a mighty clever fellow and belongs to a good family."

"Well, gentlemen, that may all be; but as for there being no one shot I know better. I have seen the man myself who was shot, and I know the man who was arrested did it."

This was a poser; they returned again to Cullen and had a long interview. This resulted in Cullen himself coming over to the hotel.

"Brown," said he, "these people all swear that nobody was shot; aint you mistaken?"

"No, captain, I am not. As I have already told you, I saw and talked with the man who is wounded, and examined his wound. That ought to set the matter at rest."

"That's so, but how am I to get rid of these people?"

"Put them all in the guard-house."

"I can't do that; they're mighty clever to me. Don't you think we'd better let him go? I'm sure he'll do nothing out of the way again."

"No, captain, that would never do. They need to be taught a lesson, and there can never be a better opportunity. This act shows a recklessness of life that needs to be curbed."

"Well, if you say so I'll keep him; but it puts me in a tight place."

"I'll telegraph to Sprague in the morning," said Brown, "and let him send up a guard to take the fellow to Jacksonville and try him there."

"By G--d, he'll hang him if he gets him there once."

"By the way, Cullen, did you put a couple of colored men in the guard-house to-night for reporting this affair to you?"

"No, sir."

"They say you did."

"If it was done I didn't know anything of it, and I don't believe it."

"Let's go down and see."

"No captain, excuse me. I don't want to see McKnight."

"Well, walk down near there with me, I want to see."

So the two walked down to a log building, a short distance outside of town. It had been used as a blacksmith shop at one time, and was not a very inviting place for a man to lodge in. A fire was burning near, around which a corporal and a few soldiers were seated; at the door was a soldier on guard. Cullen lingered behind, while Brown approached the guard and asked if two colored men had been put in there that night.

"Yes, cap'n."

"Let them come to the door."

They were called out and proved to be the comrades of Sergeant Evans. They stated that they had been put in by a lieutenant to whom they had reported the affair at the depot.

Brown walked back and consulted with Cullen. The latter then approached and gave orders for the men's release, who went on their way rejoicing.

The fire around which the corporal and his men were sitting threw some rays of light into the old shop where the prisoners were confined. Captain Brown peeped through between the logs and took a look at them. There sat McKnight on the fragment of a bench, looking the picture of rage. It was an indignity he could ill brook. Around the room were scattered a few negroes and some half-dozen soldiers. The ground was bare, with here and there a board, the only article that could be used as a bed. It looked gloomy and desolate enough.

Satisfied with his reconnaissance, he turned toward the town, and was soon joined by his companion. The two then walked silently back.

When Captain Brown reached the hotel there were still some of the crowd remaining. They again besought him to let McKnight go, using every argument that ingenuity could frame to produce an impression. He could no longer doubt that the whole responsibility of arresting the man had been thrown upon him, but he determined not to flinch. Indeed, there could be no excuse for failing to punish such an outrage. Finally, he told them it was useless to talk about the matter any longer; the man had been shot and the offense was a most unprovoked one. The party who had been arrested was the one who did it, and he would have to stand his trial for the crime. If Cullen took the responsibility of releasing him, he would report the whole matter to Colonel Sprague.

With this, he left and retired to bed.

He awakened early the next morning, and his first thoughts were of the wounded man. He determined to go down and see him and have him removed to some more comfortable quarters. Indeed, it should have been done the evening before, but in the confusion was lost sight of.

After dressing himself, he walked down toward the railroad. No one was to be seen. It was quite early, the sun not being up yet, and the air cool. On reaching the car where Sergeant Evans was the evening before, he found the door open and the place entirely empty!

Brown was completely bewildered by this new development. It was so entirely unexpected and so utterly inexplicable, that for a time he was at a loss to know what course to take.

After thinking, the matter over he concluded that some of McKnight's friends had spirited the wounded man away, in order to prevent his being used as evidence against him. Should they succeed it would also give color to the statement that the whole story about the shooting was a hoax.

He looked all round but could see no one. Finally, some distance away, on the opposite side of the railroad, he discovered two men approaching by the public road. As they came nearer, he saw that they were the ones released from the guardhouse the evening before.

Walking over to meet them, he asked:

"What has become of the sergeant?"

"Dunno," replied one of the men, "when we cum down last night thar war a hoss and a little wagon there and two men along. They had jest lifted the sergeant in and then they started on across the railroad. We followed them awhile, and saw 'em stop at a house up in the edge of the pines jest yonder," pointing to a house about a quarter of a mile away. "Then we cum back and laid in the kaw till mornin'. In the mornin' we went to see if he was there, but a man cum out and threatened to shoot us if we didn't leave, so we cum back."

This statement confirmed his suspicions, and he saw that the only way for him to do was to find the sergeant and take him direct to Jacksonville. He would have to give up for the present the purchasing of cattle and devote himself to hunting this man up and taking him away from Gainesville.

"When do the cars leave here for Jacksonville?"

"One train leaves early in de mornin', and one in de evening'."

"Well, boys, you had better get out of this. It's no place here for you any longer. I'll find the sergeant, if he is to be found, and take him down this evening. Does the railroad owe you anything?"

"Not much, cap'n. Dey owes us a little."

145

"Well, my advice to you is to settle with them and get away from here to-day. It'll be a hot place for you here when I leave."

"Yes, sah."

Brown had resolved on his course. He was determined to find the wounded man if possible, and to do it he saw that prompt action was necessary. Indeed, success depended entirely on that. So he started once more for the headquarters of the post. Every energy was now fully aroused. He had become a good deal attached to Sergeant Evans, such an attachment as a man will form for one, regardless of rank, color, or caste, who shows in his daily acts those true qualities of manliness that are as rare as they are valuable.

Reaching the place, he inquired for Captain Cullen, and was told he was in bed. He then inquired for the orderly sergeant, and was directed to his quarters. To him he told his business and asked for two horses and an orderly.

After some delay these were obtained, and armed, each with a revolver, they started. Reaching the house that had been pointed out by the negroes, Brown dismounted, and, knocking at the door, called for the proprietor.

A long, lank, cadaverous-looking fellow made his appearance, glanced cautiously at the captain's uniform, and said "good-mornin'."

"Good-morning; where is the man who was brought here last night? The man who was wounded and afterward hauled over here?"

"'Clar to God I dunno, cap'n. I can't tell whar he is."

"I want no trifling. I know there was a wounded man brought here last night. Where is he?"

"Well, there was a man brot here last night. Some men brought him here an left him in the nigger-quarters over thar. This mornin' they come an tuk him away. I don't know whar he's gone."

"Which direction did they go with him?"

"Right up the road thar, cap'n. They went about an hour ago."

Brown was satisfied that the man was now telling the truth, so he again mounted his horse and started off in the direction indicated.

The country there is very sandy, and it is difficult, indeed impossible, to follow the track of a wagon. The only chance of doing so is to observe closely, and you may see here and there where it has passed.

After they had gone about half a mile another house was observed near the road, with negro-quarters in its rear. Careful observation did not reveal any track in that direction; they determined, however, to stop. Riding up to the door, Brown inquired of a negress if a wounded man had been brought there this morning.

"No sah, dere was not."

"Did you see a wagon pass along the road?"

"Yes sah, one pass up de road a while ago."

On they went and soon reached a long stretch of pine woods. After riding half a mile here they discovered at length a narrow road leading off nearly at right angles with the main one. There were indications that a wagon had recently passed over this, and into it they turned. Pursuing it some distance, they came to a large frame house, with the inevitable negro-quarters in its rear. They felt certain the man must be here.

The proprietor, a tall, lank fellow, with a broad-brimmed hat on, was standing near the door.

"Was there a wounded man brought here this morning?" inquired Brown.

"No, cap'n, not that I know of. Thar war no one brot here."

"I do not wish to call in question your word, but I shall look for myself," said Brown, dismounting.

147

"Well, you can look, cap'n, but thar's none here."

Supposing that if he were there at all he would be in the negro-quarters, Brown passed round to the rear of the main building. A little negro boy, without hat or shoes, was sitting down playing in the sand; he started at the sight of the stranger.

"Where's the man who was brought here wounded this morning?" said he.

"He's in dar mass'r, in the back room," said the boy, pointing to a shed in the rear of one of the quarters.

He felt now that the search was about to be crowned with success. Advancing to the door he pushed it open unceremoniously; as he did so he observed the proprietor eyeing him through the back window of the large building.

There, on a bed of cotton, in the corner of the shed, lay Sergeant Evans. He looked up as the door opened.

"Good God, cap'n, that you? I was afraid you'd never find me."

"Have they hurt you much?"

"No, not much. I feel very stiff and sore though, and can't help myself much."

"I have no time to talk to you now. You must be got back, and that quickly. Do you know the men who brought you here?"

"Yes, one of 'em. He's a brother of the man who shot me."

"Well, we must get you back."

And he went out and called the proprietor, who came out, looking anything but well pleased.

"I have found the man and I want him taken back to Gainesville. Gear up your horse and cart, and take him there at once. We won't put up with any more trifling. You lied to me when I came and if you don't do what I tell you at once, I'll have you arrested and sent to Jacksonville."

The man obeyed with apparent reluctance, but without saying a word. The idea of being sent to Jacksonville alarmed him. The Floridians all understood that Colonel Sprague was not a man to be trifled with.

The horse, a miserable bunch of bones, was brought out and hitched to a shaft cart, a quantity of waste cotton laid in the bottom and the wounded man placed on it. The Floridian then mounted his horse, his long legs nearly reaching the ground, and the party started in the direction of Gainesville.

CHAPTER XV.
MOTHER AND SON.

"My mother!--manhood's anxious brow
And sterner cares have long been mine;
Yet turn I to thee fondly now,
As when upon thy bosom's shrine
My infant griefs were gently hushed to rest
And thy low whispered prayers my slumber blessed."

No incident of any consequence occurred during the journey to Gainesville, and when the party reached there they drew up in front of Captain Cullen's head-quarters. Brown dismounted, and entering, found that officer had not yet made his appearance, though it was nearly nine o'clock. Returning, he directed the orderly to keep guard over the team and its driver, and then ascended to the captain's bed-room.

After awakening him, he related all that had transpired during the morning, and stated that the wounded man was now here, and could make his own statement if any further doubt remained in regard to how, or by whom, he had been shot.

" 'Taint worth while," said Cullen, "I 'spose the story must be true; but I didn't believe it at first. I hate it like thunder to have McKnight arrested, he's such a d--d clever fellow."

"I think, captain, he's only clever because you're in power here. If the rebs were in power and he in command here, they would use you very differently from what you use them. A man who could do such an act as he has done to an unarmed and defenseless man, can never be trusted. By the way, I want to take this man down to Jacksonville today, and the morning train has gone. Where will we keep him until I am ready to go?"

"I dunno, captain, I feel awful dull this morning Let's go down-stairs and take a little whisky."

So down-stairs they went, and another black bottle was produced. After imbibing, Cullen seemed in much better spirits. Brown observed this, and said:

"Come out and see the man your friend shot, captain; I'd like you to take a look at him."

So the two walked out to where the cart stood, with the wounded man lying in it. The sergeant was evidently suffering. The jolting of the vehicle had irritated his wound and made it painful.

Cullen declined to question him, but said he'd better be taken to the hospital. He told the orderly to go to the surgeon of the hospital and ask him to come over. He soon returned in company with that officer.

"Doctor," said Cullen, "admit this man to the hospital until this afternoon. Captain Brown intends to take him to Jacksonville. He has been shot, and his wound ought to be dressed."

The doctor made some inquiry about the man and the circumstances under which he was wounded. He then went into the office, and writing a note to the hospital steward, handed it to the orderly. The sergeant was then driven to the hospital, a short distance away, and carried in and placed on a comfortable bed. The Floridian, having accomplished his allotted task, started in no very amiable mood toward home.

Captain Brown having seen the wounded man comfortably fixed, started for the hotel. Breakfast was over, but some was speedily provided, to which he did full justice.

A considerable crowd had collected in from the country, and among them he discovered several of the men who had shown so much solicitude for McKnight's release the evening before, and had so stoutly denied that he committed the act with which he was charged.

These men were aware that it was useless longer to deny the fact of the shooting, but they had not given up the idea of effecting McKnight's release. They had now adopted the theory that the affair was an accident. Several of them approached Brown and entered into conversation.

"Good-mornin', cap'n. Goin' out to look for cattle to-day?"

"No, sir, I think not. I shall return to Jacksonville this afternoon."

"Not goin' to look for cattle at all?"

"No. I intend to take care of this man who was shot. He's not safe here, and I shall at once take him to a place where I think he is safe."

"You're mistaken, cap'n. That shooting was only an accident. The man didn't intend to shoot anybody. It was only a joke on his part."

"It was a bad kind of a joke. I have never seen such jokes practiced in civilized society. Even putting your construction on the act, it shows an utter recklessness of life, such as renders a man who would do it absolutely unsafe to run at large. I don't think the man is safe here, and I propose to take him at once to a place where he will be. Neither do I believe McKnight, who shot him, is fit to run at large. It is an offense for which he must be tried and take his chances."

"But, cap'n, he's a mighty clever fellow, and his family are among the best in Florida, and it seems purty hard that he must be tried for his life for shootin' a nigger."

"All you say may be true; but it is better for you and all concerned that every man who has no more regard for the law and for human life, than to fire into a crowd of unarmed men, should be arrested and punished, no matter how clever he is or what his family may be. As for the man he shot being a negro, that is true, but it only makes the offense greater. He imagined he could shoot a colored man with impunity, and this consideration adds cowardice to the act. Besides, the negroes were the friends of the government in its great struggle. This man was a Union soldier, served his country with fidelity, and obtained an honorable discharge."

"If it would refuse to protect him it would not deserve to exist. So far as I am concerned, I am determined to lay the whole matter before the proper authorities. If justice is not done in this instance it shall not be my fault. No consideration of any character would tempt me to be a party to hushing up the affair. It must take its course."

This closed the matter so far as any attempt to induce Brown to consent to McKnight's release was concerned. They saw it was no use to press it further.

He then walked over to Cullen's head-quarters.

"Captain," said he, "I think I will telegraph to Col. Sprague to send up a sergeant and a few men to take McKnight down to Jacksonville. He will have to be tried there."

"Well, I dunno. Let me see, hadn't I better send him down on the train with you? I'll send a guard along."

"Yes, that'll do. Perhaps it's better, because these people will annoy you so long as you have him here. By this means you'll get rid of all that trouble sooner."

"That's what I was thinking; I'll have no peace as long as I have him here."

Brown then walked over to the hospital.

He met the surgeon just outside the door. "Well, doctor, how's our patient? have you examined his wound?"

"Captain," said the surgeon, who seemed to be a very careful and humane man, "there is something singular about that man's wound. The ball struck him high up on the hip and evidently glanced. I cannot find it. It has gone somewhere, and may do him no harm, but still I am afraid. You must put him under the charge of a skillful surgeon when you get to Jacksonville. His case may prove worse than we anticipate."

"I have no doubt the post-surgeon there will take charge of him. This man is a discharged Union soldier, and I feel sure there will be no trouble. If there should be, there's a freedman's hospital there, and a good surgeon has charge of it, who will no doubt be willing to do whatever he can."

"What a fine looking man this negro is. He seems to be quite intelligent too."

"Yes. I suppose he has had better opportunities than they generally have."

"Where's he from?"

"Philadelphia. His mother is living there now. He thinks a great deal of her; his father is dead, and there's no other children. It'll be rough on her if he goes off this way after coming safe through the war."

"Better write for her to come down and take care of him. He may be hurt internally, though I ain't sure. At any rate I don't believe he will be well very soon. This moving about does him no good; but it can't be helped. If his mother was to come she'd take better care of him than anybody else; besides, if anything should happen she'd be better satisfied at being here."

"That's true. I'll speak to him about it."

So the two walked in and entered into conversation with Sergeant Evans. After talking some time about his wound and other matters connected with it, Brown said.

"When did you last hear from your mother, sergeant?"

"Not for a month. I ought to write to her, too; havn't written for some time."

"Wouldn't it be a good plan to have her come down to Jacksonville? You'll need be taken care of for some time, and nobody will do it as well as she."

He looked startled. Turning toward the doctor, he inquired:

"Doctor, do you imagine this wound can be dangerous?"

"No, I think not. Still, it may require a long time to get well;" and he added hesitatingly: "it often happens that in such cases here the patient takes chills and fever, and requires care and good nursing for a long while."

The sergeant fell into a deep study, and at length said:

"I'll send for her. Mother would like to come down here, anyway; and if she knows there's anything the matter with me, she'll have no peace at home.

Sergeant Evans had saved considerable money during his term of service in the army, which he had placed, before coming to Gainesville, in the hands of a Northern merchant who was doing business at Jacksonville. Brown knew this and asked:

"Had you better send her some money? It'll take considerable to pay her passage down."

"No; mother has the means to come. She owns a small house, and always has some money ahead," pursued the sergeant, with a look of satisfaction. "I'll only have to send her word. When does the steamer go out, cap'n?"

"To-morrow morning. We'll be down in time to send a letter by it."

Steamers plied between Savannah and Jacksonville twice a week. These conveyed mails and passengers between Florida and the North. There were regular lines of steamers between Savannah and the ports of Philadelphia and New York.

"He might as well write the letter now," remarked the doctor. After you get down, there might not be time, nor so good an opportunity."

So he obtained paper, pen and ink, and one of the nurses was directed to bring a table and place it by the bedside. Thus provided, he leaned over and slowly and somewhat painfully, for he was suffering from the wound, indited the epistle.

While thus engaged something in his appearance attracted Brown's attention and puzzled him. He had not observed it before, nor could he satisfy himself exactly what it was, nor why it should particularly impress him. It was an expression of countenance of a peculiar and striking character that could not be well described by words. The mystery about it was that it carried back his thoughts to some almost forgotten period of the past, and awakened memories that had been still and silent for years. And yet, these were so vague and undefined, so apparently unreal, that he could make nothing out of them. He struggled with these thoughts a few minutes, and seemed on the very verge of catching up some important thread that would lead to a solution of the mystery, and then it was lost more hopelessly than ever in the deep'ning shadows of the past. Worried and perplexed, at length he dismissed it from his mind entirely.

"Give me the letter, sergeant, and I'll see that it goes off in the steamer to-morrow morning."

Sergeant Evans, who was just writing the direction, finished it and handed the letter over, which Brown placed in his pocket.

The doctor and Captain Brown now departed, and the latter directed his footsteps toward the depot. Here he found the men who had been released from the guard-house on the previous evening.

"Good-morning, cap'n."

"Well, boys, have you settled up your affairs here and prepared to leave?"

"Yes, cap'n, de man paid us and we're ready to go."

"Do they owe the sergeant anything?"

"Dunno, I guess dey does tho'."

"Where is the agent?"

"In de little box over yonder. He's got de office dar," pointing to a little office some distance away, about four feet square, and made of pine boards nailed on a rough frame.

Brown passed over and entered. The agent was a man apparently about thirty, and did not have the appearance of a native. He looked like one who knew something about his business and attended to it.

Brown inquired concerning his account with the sergeant, and was told they owed him twenty dollars. He asked if they would pay the money to him, and, after relating the circumstances, was told that they would. It was suggested, however, that the sergeant could sign a receipt, and one of the negroes was called and dispatched with one to him for that purpose. He soon returned, and the money was paid over.

He and the agent then fell into conversation on the occurrences of the previous evening and the general condition of society in Florida.

"The white people around here," remarked the latter, "at least the most of them, are continually complaining about the laziness of the negroes and their disinclination to work. The fact is, that with a few rare exceptions, they are the only ones who will work. A pretty time we'd have here if they were as lazy as the whites! It's bad enough as it is, but in that case it would be infinitely worse. The young white men of this State are as worthless a set of fellows as there is upon the face of the earth. This fellow, McKnight, is a bad, dangerous man, and a curse to the neighborhood. The gang who go with him are but little better, though none of them are quite as reckless as he. They are all the worse for belonging to so-called good families, and possessing some mental culture and education. It would be hard to imagine a more dangerous class, and one more difficult to manage."

"Do the respectable citizens, men of age and character, countenance their conduct?"

"Well, no, not exactly; but still they are their apologists. The fact is, the existence of slavery in this country demoralized everybody. The blacks were looked upon as mere brutes, and absolutely subject to their masters. The great change which has taken place is distasteful even to the best citizens here. They hate the negro because he has obtained his freedom, and because he has the same legal rights with themselves. You'll find that they'll never get over it."

"Wouldn't it be dangerous for you to express such convictions here, openly?"

"Of course. I never do it except where I know it is safe. I know it is safe with you, because I know all about your connection with this case."

"Do the military authorities here execise any influence in preserving order and in protecting the negroes?"

"Not much. They ought to, but do not. Look, for instance, at this man Cullen. What protection does he give to the negroes? Why, if you had not been here McKnight would not have been arrested for shooting Evans. Not long since he actually had a negro tied to a tree and whipped, by a soldier, on complaint of a white man in the neighborhood. The negro refused to work, alleging that he could get no wages. Complaint was made to the commander of this post, who had him tied up and whipped."

"Is that possible? He must have been drunk."

"Quite likely; but when was he ever sober? I'm sure not long at a time. You'll find that the moment you leave he'll release McKnight, and there'll be no more of it. He'll not be in the guardhouse an hour after you leave."

"Well, we've provided for that. We are going to take him along."

"I'm glad to hear it. I hope he'll never come back. This place will be well rid of him."

"Are you a native of this State?"

"Yes, I was born here. My father, though, was a Massachusetts man and came to Florida when quite young. He married here, and was for many years engaged in the lumber business, at which he made a good deal of money. He often thought of going back to his native State; but the remembrance of its severe winters deterred him, so he lingered in this sunny clime until the rebellion came and it was too late. He never held a slave, and worked with his own hands on a plantation near here. I suppose I have imbibed his feelings and opinions, though he has always been exceedingly careful about expressing them."

"Were you in the rebel service?"

"Yes; I was telegraph operator for them. I had been in that business years before. After the war was over, I obtained this position here."

"Did you believe in their cause?"

"No, I did not. I never was even a defender of slavery. But I had either to go in the capacity I did or carry a musket. I preferred the former. If I had undertaken to keep out of the rebel army, I would have been obliged to hide myself in the woods with the chances of being shot. So I went in."

"Well, said Brown, "I must leave you. I am glad to have met you and heard your views in relation to the condition of things here. Good morning."

He proceeded to the hotel, where he remained until some time after dinner, and then went again to the hospital. Here he made arrangements with the doctor to have the sergeant conveyed to the station in ample time for the evening train. He then called upon Captain Cullen.

Cullen was in his office with an agent of the Freedmen's Bureau, who had just arrived from Tallahassee. He had come by private conveyance and was looking after the interests of the freedmen in that region. He was assisting the commandant of the post to demolish a bottle of Wilson's whisky. Both were already quite sensible of its effects, and were discussing affairs of State with great animation.

"They o't never t' 'av' set the niggers free," said Cullen. "I never tho't 't was constitutional."

"Twarn't," replied the agent, who had been a lieutenant in the invalid corps, "but it can't be help'd now. But they'll have to keep straight. I b'lieve Johnson'll keep 'em up to the chalk line. I tell ye he's down on Radicals."

"Bully fellow, Andy is," replied Cullen, with a knowing look, "I've took many a drink with him in Tennessee. None 'o yer babies he ain't. I tell ye he can take a snorter."

"Captain Cullen," interposed Brown, "I am going to start in the train which leaves here at four o'clock. You stated your intention of sending down the prisoner, McKnight, under guard, to Jacksonville. Will you have him at the depot in time to go by that train so that I can take charge of him?" Brown thought he detected a slight change in the captain's countenance, but he replied promptly:

"Yes, sir, I'll have him there. I want to send him in the train you go in."

The doctor in charge of the hospital sent Sergeant Evans to the depot some twenty minutes before the time for the starting of the train. He had made all necessary provision for his comfort. A narrow straw bed was provided for him to lay on, and a government blanket to cover him. The train consisted of two rickety old passenger cars and a half dozen freight cars loaded with cotton. Behind these was one entirely empty, which was being sent back to Jacksonville, and into it the wounded man was lifted. His two comrades were allowed to occupy it with him.

The train would now start in ten minutes, and still neither Captain Cullen nor the guard with the prisoner made their appearance. Brown began to feel uneasy, and remembered the expression on the captain's countenance when he had mentioned the matter in the afternoon. He went to the agent and asked if Cullen had applied for transportation for the prisoner and guard.

"Yes, sir," was the reply, "he notified me an hour ago that they were to be sent down on this train."

This made him feel easy, and he waited a few minutes longer. Still no one appeared, and the train would start in a few minutes. He then asked the conductor to detain it ten minutes. This was not an unusual thing on Southern railroads, and that official readily consented. A soldier, who was at the station, was dispatched to head-quarters to ascertain if they were coming. He returned and said they would be there "in two minutes." This gave fresh hope, but ten minutes elapsed and they did not come--so the train moved off.

Captain Brown felt that he had been badly sold; but there seemed to be no remedy. Evidently, Cullen had not intended to send the prisoner down at all, and in all probability would release him. He had invented the plan in order to prevent intelligence from being transmitted to Colonel Sprague, and did not intend that the prisoner should pass into his hands. The only thing that could be done now was to lay the whole matter before the latter officer.

The train arrived at Jacksonville after dark, and the wounded man was carried into the dwelling of a colored man near by, to remain until morning, when permanent quarters could be secured. His comrades remained to take care of him.

Captain Brown sought the quarters of Colonel Sprague and laid the whole matter before him. Beginning with his first arrival at Gainesville, he related all that had occurred until he left, and how he had intended to telegraph concerning the affair, but had been deceived by a promise that the prisoner would be sent down on the train.

When he had concluded, the commandant of the District of Florida was in a high state of excitement. He walked the floor of his office back and forth, considerably agitated, swearing vigorously. At length he said:

"Such a state of things is perfectly damnable; but what am I to do? The government requires me to keep up all these posts, and each one must have a commissioned officer. I hav'nt enough to fill them all now, and keep what are needed here. This man ought to be dismissed from the service at once, and I would do it if I had any one to take his place; but I hav'nt, so I must keep him."

"Orderly," said the colonel, "I want you to go to the telegraph office. Here, I'll send a dispatch," and he wrote off a dispatch and handed it to him.

The orderly started off, but soon returned with the intelligence that they could get no answer from Gainesville, the office being closed.

"Then," said the colonel, "we can accomplish nothing to-night. I'll send up early in the morning."

In the morning word was received from Gainesville that McKnight had escaped from the guardhouse. Everybody who knew anything about the affair believed he was purposely let go, but the affair was allowed to die out without an investigation.

Sergeant Evans was not admitted to the post hospital at Jacksonville, as not being in the service he could not be, by the rules, but was placed in a freedman's hospital which had been, some time previously, established there. He remained there,

however, but a few days, and was taken to a private house, belonging to a well-to-do colored man of the town, situated near the outskirts, where he had all the comfort and attention that could be bestowed on him, at a comparatively trifling cost.

Dr. H. Byrne, surgeon of the post, a most excellent and amiable man, at the instance of Captain Brown, with whom he was well acquainted, consented to take charge of his case, and gave him every attention.

His case seemed a very peculiar one. The bullet had evidently penetrated to some point where it was doing him a serious injury and might prove fatal; but exactly where that was the surgeon could not determine. To add to the difficulty of his case, he was attacked with chills and fever, the prevailing disease of the region, and was gradually growing weaker and thinner. Dr. Byrne seemed much puzzled with his case, and evidently contemplated the possibility of an unfavorable termination.

Still he was cheerful, and could sit up and occasionally take some nourishment. He conversed freely, and looked forward anxiously to the arrival of his mother.

"I told her in the letter to inquire for you, cap'n," said he one day to Brown, "I knew she could find your office very easy."

"That was right. I'll bring her up when she comes."

Some two weeks after the return from Gainesville, Brown was seated in his office near the wharf, where the steamers that brought the Northern mails and passengers landed, when he heard the shrill whistle of a steamer, and looking out at the window, saw the "Cosmopolitan" approaching. There was a general rush toward the wharf, and in a few minutes the newsboys were crying "Tribune" and "Herald" through the streets, these being the only Northern papers the people cared to read. Providing himself with a Tribune, he began to look over the news.

The day was pleasant and the door of the office stood partly open. Presently a colored woman, neatly dressed, came up to it, and looking cautiously in, inquired:

"Is this Cap'n Brown's office?"

"Yes, ma'am," was the reply. "Come in."

Stepping cautiously inside the door she again inquired:

"Are you Cap'n Brown?"

"Yes, ma'am."

"Can you tell me where I can find Sergeant Evans?"

"Yes, I can; are you his mother?"

"Yes, sir."

"Well, come in and sit down. I'll send some one to show you the way."

The woman came in and took a seat in a quiet and undemonstrative manner. She was well up in life, probably sixty years old, but still vigorous and active. Her complexion was of a dark brown, and her face bore marks of great strength of character.

Her eye was large and earnest, and her general air that of one who, whatever her hand might find to do, done it with all her might. Captain Brown observed a striking resemblance between her and her son.

"Cap'n" said she, in a low, earnest voice, "how is the sergeant?"

"He's still poorly; I hope he's not dangerous."

Brown sent a negro, who often attended to such business, on board the boat to get the woman's baggage, for which she had a check. Feeling some curiosity to witness the meeting of mother and son, he determined to accompany her himself. So he told her he would go with her and show her where the sergeant was.

Up through the streets of the town, over the plank walks to the outskirts, and then through the sand, ankle-deep, they went. At length they reached a neat frame house with water-oaks and maples in front, and here they paused. Brown told the woman to remain outside while be entered an prepared her son for the interview. She made no answer, but stood motionless. Opening the door of the room, he passed in. Sergeant Evans was lying in bed and looked emaciated and careworn The moment he saw Captain Brown's face, he said, eagerly:

"I heard the steamer's whistle, cap'n; has mother come?"

"Yes, she is here. Shall I bring her in?"

"Oh, yes, let her come in."

The door was opened and the woman entered. The moment he saw her he stretched out his arms, eagerly, like a child, and cried, "Oh! mother!"

She tottered forward to the bedside, sank in his arms, and covering his face with kisses, sobbed out, "Oh! Charley, Charley, my God! is this you?"

CHAPTER XVI.
HOME AT LAST.

"Our lives are rivers gliding free
To that unfathom'd, boundless sea,
The silent grave!
Thither all earthly pomp and boast
Roll, to be swallowed up and lost
In one dark wave."

CAPTAIN BROWN passed quietly out of the room, and closing the door, left mother and son by themselves. The negro just at that moment came up with the trunk, and inquired what he should do with it. He was directed to leave it on the porch, and Brown gave him fifty cents, with which he went on his way rejoicing.

As he stepped down from the porch, he glanced carelessly at the direction on the trunk. It was written in a large, plain hand, and could be read at a distance readily: "Mary Evans, Jacksonville, Florida."

"Poor woman," he muttered to himself, as he closed the yard-gate, and started toward home. "I'm afraid she'll never see her son in the North again; he looks badly to-day."

The sergeant seemed to be gradually wearing out. Day by day he grew thinner and weaker, and the utmost skill of his physician appeared to be of no avail. Poor fellow! he bore up nobly and never gave any indications of despair, but his friends began to feel that his case was not an encouraging one, and feared the worst.

As Brown passed near Dr. Byrne's quarters, he determined to drop in and hear his opinion again concerning his patient. He had heard it twenty times before, but hoped, without any good reason, that this time it might be more favorable. So he turned in toward the snug little frame house where the doctor could always be found when not on duty, and was informed by an orderly that he was inside.

So, being on intimate terms, he walked in, and found Dr. Byrne deep in the mysteries of the Tribune.

"Well, doctor, I've just been taking some medicine to one of your patients; thought I'd stop and let you know."

"What patient?"

"Sergeant Evans."

"What medicine have you been taking him?"

"His mother."

"Ha! ha!" looking slightly relieved, "I'm glad of that; I'm right glad she's come," laying down the Tribune on a small pine table close by; "the sergeant has been worrying himself about her, and I think it has contributed to prevent his improvement. Do you know, Brown, that I have been somewhat discouraged about his case of late?"

"I feared as much."

"It is one of those cases," resumed the doctor, "in which medical skill can do nothing beyond keeping up healthy conditions as much as possible, and trusting to nature for the result."

"When do you intend to see him again?"

"To-morrow morning. It is now near four o'clock, and I cannot go to-day."

"By the way, doctor," said Brown, "did you ever meet anything in your career that seemed to sharpen your recollection of long-past events and carry you, seemingly, to the very verge of remembering something important, connected, apparently, with that which set in motion this new current of thought, and yet stubbornly refused to enlighten you any further; leaving you floundering between the known and unknown in a most uncomfortable and ludicrous position?"

"No, sir; but pray, why do you ask?"

"Because I find myself in just such a predicament. I have no reason to believe I ever saw Sergeant Evans until I came to Florida, a few months ago; nor have I the slightest reason for believing I ever laid eyes upon his mother until after the arrival of the 'Cosmopolitan' this afternoon, but there is something about him, and also something about her, that is forever reminding me of things that are on the very verge of memory, that float over and hover about the boundary line between the known and unknown, and seem to be on the point of taking up a connecting thread between the present and the past; but it is never quite reached. What is it?"

"It's nonsense, Brown, an article that you're never at a loss for," said the doctor, indulging in a hearty laugh. "I wouldn't be surprised now if that was some vague notion you'd gathered up in that book I saw laying on your table the other day. What's this its title is? 'Footsteps on the Boundary of Another World?' Well, there's where it came from. There's nothing in it, Brown; no, sir! not a thing."

"Well, I think differently," said Brown, a good deal annoyed by this unexpected reception of his pet theory, "but time will show who's right."

"Of course it will," laughed the doctor, "it always does. But I've noticed it never shows much favor to these vague, undefined dreams or baseless theories, and I s'pose it won't soon begin. But, Brown, that sergeant seems to be a noble fellow. I've taken a strong liking to him, and have done all in my power, and will continue to do all I can, to help him through. I never met with a negro to whom I was so favorably inclined. What kind of a woman does his mother seem to be?"

"Very much like him. There's a striking resemblance between the two."

"Aye, that's it then, the old story. I believe every man that has anything in him worth while gets it from his mother. Well, I'm glad she's here. It can't help but do him some good."

The conversation here ended, and Brown left, while the doctor wended his way to the hospital to make his usual afternoon rounds among the patients.

Early the next forenoon Brown directed his footsteps toward the house where Sergeant Evans and his mother were. Just before he reached the house Doctor Byrne came out; as they met he said:

"Good-morning, Brown; going in to see our patient? I think the medicine you brought has improved him."

"I'm glad to hear it, doctor. I'll go in and see how he looks."

Opening the door quietly, he saw the sick man, well propped up with pillows, looking happier than he had done for some days past. The room looked neat and cheerful, and a vase of beautiful flowers stood in the window near his bedside.

His mother had evidently taken a good deal of pains to make everything as comfortable and home-like as possible; and considering the limited means at her command, had succeeded admirably.

Still she did not look cheerful, though evidently struggling to appear so. It was apparent that she had found her son in much worse condition than she had expected.

After inquiring of the sergeant how he had passed the night, and talking awhile with the woman concerning her voyage, Brown asked if she was a native of Philadelphia.

"No, sir. I was born in Maryland."

"Were you a slave there, Mrs. Evans?"

The woman hesitated; for years upon years she had been so reticent on this subject that even now, when she knew the necessity for it had passed away, she at first declined to speak of her former condition. She recovered from this, however, in a few minutes, and said:

"Yes, sir, I was a slave; but my husband and I escaped into Pennsylvania some thirty-five years ago. Charley, there, was a little child, scarcely more than a year old, and him I carried in my arms for many a weary night. I never would have got away though except for one blessed old man that lived over in Pennsylvania, near the line."

"What part of Pennsylvania?" inquired Brown, his curiosity now excited.

"In Lancaster county."

"In Lancaster county? are you sure?" asked Brown, a little incredulously. "I'm from Lancaster county myself."

"Yes, sir, he lived in Lancaster county. We crossed the river at Conowingo bridge. I've looked at the map a thousand times since, and can't be mistaken."

"And who was this old man you speak of," inquired Brown, his curiosity now raised to the highest pitch.

"Davy McCann."

Brown started from his chair and glared at the woman for a moment almost incredulously; but it was for a moment only. With the speed of thought that magic name carried his memory back into the almost forgotten past, and, unlocking its portals, revealed long past events in undimmed distinctness. Walking across the floor a few times in deep thought, he turned to the woman and asked:

"Is your name Mary?"

"Yes, sir."

"Was your husband's name John?"

"Yes, sir."

"Are you the woman that Davy. McCann brought to Brown's, at Brown's fording, one dark night about thirty-five years ago, with your husband and a little child?"

"Yes, sir."

"Is that the boy?" pointing to the sergeant.

"Yes, sir."

"And you remember of sitting on the cellar steps in the old kitchen, with Charley clasped in your arms, while the people from camp-meeting were passing by, almost frightened to death for fear some of them were after you?"

"Yes, sir," answered the woman, now beginning to look as much surprised as her questioner.

"And were you captured while there, and rescued?"

"Oh, yes. I remember all that; but how do you come to know anything about it?"

"Do you remember a little boy, about five or six years old, at Brown's while you were there?"

"Yes, sir. His name was Frank."

"Well, you're looking at him now. I'm that boy."

The woman seemed utterly bewildered, and could only exclaim, "'Fore God!" and sank back in a chair.

Brown remembered his conversation with Doctor Byrne the previous afternoon, and exulting in the vindication of his theory, which to-day's revelation had brought out, determined to seek out that individual and give him a surprise. So he bade the sergeant and his mother good-morning, and made his way to the doctor's quarters.

He was, as usual, engaged in reading when his friend entered. Looking up, he inquired of Brown what he thought of the sergeant now?

Without seeming to hear the remark at all, that individual broke out:

"See here, old fellow, what do think of 'vague theories,' 'baseless dreams' and all such like? Nothing in 'em, ever, I 'spose? Of course there aint. Mind what you said yesterday? I told you time would show. So it has. Just listen to me;" and he sat down and rattled off the whole story as learned from the woman a short time before.

The doctor listened attentively, and with evident interest. When his voluble friend had concluded, he remarked:

"Well, this is all very interesting, indeed; but there is nothing mysterious in your having some idea that you had met or seen these people before. The recollection of some peculiar expression of countenance was fixed in your memory, and though blurred and rendered indistinct by the lapse of time, only required some well-defined fact with which that recollection was associated to bring it out clearly and plainly. But, leaving that out of the question, this is really a remarkable affair. Many a highly-wrought romance has been founded on far less substantial foundation. You should go to work and write it out."

"Yes, it's likely I'd do that. A fellow who hardly has patience to write a letter."

"Well, get some one else to do it. There's certainly a fine opportunity here."

With this remark the two parted, Brown going to his office, where he remained until late in the afternoon.

Toward evening he again wended his way to the sick man's quarters. He felt a new interest in the fate of these people, whom accident had thrown so strangely, and at periods so remote from each other, across his track. He determined to learn something of their history during the intervening time.

Seating himself, he asked Mary if she would relate the principal events that had happened to her and the kind of life she had led since the night she and John and the little boy started out into the darkness with Davy McCann, so many years ago. The woman seemed quite willing to comply, and seating herself, made, in substance, the following statement:

"After we left Brown's that night we traveled as rapidly as we could in a north-easterly direction. We used public roads but little; but went on through woods and fields, following by-paths with which Davy seemed perfectly familiar. Indeed, sometimes there was not even a path to guide us; but he was never at a loss, going straight on while we followed. Near morning we stopped at a farm-house, and the old man called up the owner and told him who we were. He had frequently stopped there before, and we were at once made welcome. The people proved to be Quakers, and soon provided us with an ample meal and put us to bed, where we slept away most of the day. The next night the same thing was repeated, and we reached a house toward morning situated somewhere in Bucks county. The people here were also Quakers. Here our connection with Davy McCann ceased. I heard some years after that he was dead, and felt that I had lost my best friend on earth.

"We got places to work in this neighborhood, and began to feel pretty secure and comfortable, but during the winter which followed, John, my husband, took sick and died. He had a severe attack of inflammation of the lungs, and not being very strong, sunk under it."

Here Mary paused, and dropping a tear, was silent for a few moments. Resuming the thread of her narrative, she said that she remained here for nearly a year, and was much attached to the lady who was her employer. It happened, however, that the woman's sister, who was connected with the management of a large female boarding-school in the vicinity of Philadelphia, came up there on a visit, and taking a fancy to Mary, asked her to come and live with her, promising her good wages, and in addition, to learn her the common branches of education.

This was a temptation not to be resisted, for above all things she longed to know how to read and write. So with her employer's consent she accompanied this lady to her pleasant and beautiful home near the city.

Here she remained for many years, and not only learned to read and write, but formed quite a taste for literary acquirements. Her constant contact with persons of good education had also a perceptible effect on her mind and conversation, and she fell gradually into the habit of using such language as prevailed in society of that character.

During her residence here she accumulated considerable means. She received very good wages, all of which she saved; besides, she received many presents from the boarders, all of whom were kind to her.

Here Charley, also, had a fine opportunity to obtain an education, which he improved by every means in his power. When they left he was sixteen years of age, and had what would be called anywhere a good common education.

During all this time they had never been molested by slave-hunters, and, indeed, the fear of it had almost entirely passed away.

After remaining here for nearly fifteen years, the good woman who had employed her sickened and died, and Mary felt that she was again nearly alone in the world.

But an acquaintance of the woman's, residing in the city, who had often seen Mary, and knew her value, urgently solicited her to come and live with her, to which she at length consented.

Here she remained for many years, while Charley obtained a situation as laborer at a large wholesale house, where he gave excellent satisfaction and received good wages.

After some years, however, Mary grew weary of constant labor; so she and Charley purchased, with their combined earnings, a comfortable little home in the outskirts of the city, to which she removed. Here she did washing and ironing, and made a good living. Charley boarded with her and things went on as pleasantly as they well could do.

So the world found them at the breaking out of the war. They took the papers and read them carefully, and understood fully the causes which brought it about. She felt that the time had come at last to strike the death-blow to slavery, but oh! it was more than she could bear that her son should be one to fill the breach.

But as time rolled on, and the red tide of war surged back and forth, and doubt and division began to arise in the North, and the necessity for arming the colored people became apparent, she began to feel that even he was not too precious a gift to lay upon the altar of freedom.

So when they began to enlist colored troops in Philadelphia, Charley joined them, with his mother's consent, and left for the seat of war with her most fervent blessings.

"I never was a praying woman before, cap'n," said she in conclusion, "but after he left me I sometimes spent whole nights on my knees. When the war was over, and I knew he was safe through it, I felt as though I never could thank God enough."

Silence fell on the group when Mary ended her story. The deep'ning shadows of evening gradually thickened into the darker curtain of night, and the sick man, weak and weary, fell asleep. Without a word Brown noiselessly opened the door and passed out into the darkness.

Days passed, as they will, swiftly away. The wounded man grew thinner and weaker, and Dr. Byrne at length reluctantly told his friend that there was no hope. The mother asked no questions, and made no sign; but her instincts, deeper and truer than the physician's art, told her that her son was dying. Still she relaxed no exertion. More tenderly than ever, with a closer industry and a more untiring hand she barred every approach of the king of terrors. Every morning, by daylight, it mattered not whether sleep had visited her eyelids, she could be found in the little market-house by the river side, selecting the choicest and finest oranges for Charley. Through the long days she watched his every movement, attended to the slightest want, and studied every opportunity for his comfort. As he grew weak and almost helpless, he relied upon her as wholly as though he were an infant.

Late one afternoon, in the month of February, Capt. Brown was making his way to the house where Sergeant Evans lay. Meeting Dr. Byrne some distance from the place, he observed an unusual expression on his countenance. Not venturing to ask what it meant he merely looked an inquiry.

"He's dying," said the doctor, and passed on. Brown soon reached the house and entered. It needed no second look to verify the doctor's statement. The sergeant was indeed dying. The last day or two had wrought a fearful change in his appearance. Still he was sensible and knew those around him. The proprietor of the house, with his wife and two or three colored persons, were in the room. Looking up, as Brown came in, he murmured, "Good-bye, cap'n, I'm going," and made a faint effort to hold out his hand. Brown approached and took it, but he had no word to utter.

His mother sat by the bedside on a chair, her hand resting in his, and her eyes never for a moment leaving his face. She looked the picture of cold, stony despair; but her lips uttered no sound, and her eye was as dry as the sands of the desert. For some time the dying man lay still, apparently sleeping. At length his eyes slowly opened, and rested for a moment steadily on his mother's face, an expression almost angelic flitted across his countenance, and he faintly murmured, "Mother."

This was too much for Mary, and reaching over she pressed her lips frantically against his fore-head, now almost cold. A convulsive shiver passed over his frame, his chest heaved, his eye grew dim, and there was silence--he was dead.

On a hill-side sloping northward from the town, in a neat inclosure, where reposed the dead heroes of the Union army, Sergeant Evans was buried. Clothed in his soldier's uniform, with the flag of his country wrapped around him, he was laid silently and sorrowfully away. Many citizens of the place and a number of officers of the Federal army followed him to his final resting-place. His mother was there, and the kind-hearted colored people of the place gave her every attention, but she seemed to heed it not. Her heart was in the grave with her fondly-loved and ever-to-be-remembered Charley.

After the funeral she seemed to droop, and gave evidence of rapidly declining health. She uttered no complaint, nor did she speak of her loss; but twice every day she visited his grave and busied herself with planting beautiful flowers on that sacred spot. Captain Brown suggested to her one day the idea of returning North; but she scarcely noticed his remark.

Dr. Byrne visited her frequently and gave her occasionally some medicine, though he had but little confidence in it doing her any good. Day by day she grew weaker, but still she tottered back and forth, morning and evening, to the spot that to her was the most sacred on earth, each day's journey carrying her nearer home. At length the turning-point was reached, and the long-suffering and noble woman sank beneath her griefs. Peacefully as a child she entered the dark valley, and looking forward with earnest gaze into the gathering gloom, her lips murmured "Charley," and closed forever.

Gently and lovingly, the people who had learned to love and respect her, laid her beside her son. There the two noble hearts repose. Through turmoil and trouble, through perils and dangers, with hearts untainted, happy rather as the victims than the doers of wrong, they have reached HOME AT LAST.

THE END.

www.ingramcontent.com/pod-product-compliance
Lightning Source LLC
Chambersburg PA
CBHW081329090426
42737CB00017B/3061